Drama and English at the Heart of the Curriculum

Drama and English at the Heart of the Curriculum

Primary and Middle Years

JOE WINSTON

 David Fulton Publishers

David Fulton Publishers
2 Park Square, Milton Park, Abingdon, Oxon OX14 4RN

270 Madison Avenue, New York, NY 10016

First published in Great Britain in 2004 by David Fulton Publishers
Transferred to digital printing

David Fulton Publishers is an imprint of the Taylor & Francis Group, an informa business

Copyright © Joe Winston 2004

Note: The right of Joe Winston to be identified as the author of this work has been asserted by
him in accordance with the Copyright, Designs and Patents Act 1988.

British Library Cataloguing in Publication Data
A catalogue record for this book is available from the British Library.

ISBN 1 84312 059 3

Typeset by Servis Filmsetting Ltd, Manchester

Contents

Introduction

It's these little things, they can pull you under,
Live your life filled with joy and wonder
                    'Sweetness Follows', REM

This book is intended for all teachers and student teachers interested in using drama to make their teaching more creative. It developed from a series of projects taught in a variety of schools in the West Midlands and South-west of England in 2003. All the projects were planned and taught in partnership with class teachers who had a responsibility for language and literacy in their particular schools.

In choosing the schools and in planning, teaching and evaluating the projects, I had a number of aims in mind. First and foremost, I wanted the work to be exciting, challenging and enjoyable for the children. I wanted it to be integrated closely into the broad English curriculum, to stimulate oracy, of course, but also reading and writing activities. I also wanted to explore how drama could be seen to work across the curriculum, linking with foundation subjects such as history, geography and science but, more specifically, with certain areas of the curriculum that are cross-curricular in nature – citizenship, spirituality, Information and Communications Technology (ICT) and creativity. Finally, I wanted the schools and the classrooms to be different, so that more specifically contextualised issues could emerge from the work. One class had a high proportion of children with learning difficulties; one a significant number of children who spoke English as an Additional Language; one class drew 80 per cent of its children from British South Asian communities and one was in a school recently placed in serious weaknesses after an Ofsted inspection. All the projects were carefully documented, through videotaped lessons, interviews with groups of children and with the teachers themselves and, when relevant, with support services.

The book that has emerged is intended to be at once practical and theoretical, the theory being grounded in and related directly to the practice. Chapter 1 presents my personal vision of what constitutes good drama teaching for children between the ages of 5 and 13.[1] Chapter 2 offers an argument for seeing drama as integral to successful language learning in primary and middle schools, drawing examples from the projects themselves. Chapters 3 to 6 outline the projects in detail, as schemes of work, providing specific links to nationally agreed objectives in English and the National Curriculum. Each of the schemes is accompanied by an essay which critically examines drama's potential contribution to children's education in the areas of citizenship, spirituality, ICT and creativity respectively. Chapter 7 begins by offering advice on assessment before examining specific issues that emerged from evaluating the projects in their particular contexts. These context-specific issues are important, I believe, as they acknowledge that, although teaching happens within a unique combination of circumstances, there are nonetheless stories that emerge from these instances that are worth sharing with fellow professionals because of the significance that resonates from the issues they involve.

I have not presumed any previous knowledge of drama teaching on the part of the reader. The schemes of work are presented as step-by-step guides with easy-to-follow explanations to enable you to copy or adapt them at will. The brief appendices are specifically intended to provide support for those of you new to using drama as part of your teaching. But the book is intended as more than another beginner's guide to drama teaching, to do more than demonstrate how drama can support nationally prescribed objectives in literacy and learning. It begins from an optimistic vision of teachers and student teachers. It respects their intellectual curiosity and their professional commitment, seeing them as necessarily capable of independent and creative thinking and not simply as skilful but compliant respondents to government directives. It assumes a broad educational vision on their part, one that embraces a desire to see children succeed academically and socially and also a desire to bring some joy and a sense of wonder into their lives. Hence the short quote at the beginning of this introduction. To bring joy and wonder into teaching and learning is, I believe, a noble ambition and one that I am happy to aspire to.

Note

1 Throughout the text I refer to 'primary children' and 'primary teachers' rather than 'primary and middle school children/teachers'.

Acknowledgements

I would like to acknowledge my thanks and indebtedness to the staff and pupils of the following schools:

Cubbington C of E Primary School, Warwickshire

Edgewick Primary School, Coventry

Haywards Primary School, Crediton, Devon

Stoke Hill First School, Exeter, Devon

I would also like to thank the following individuals whose ideas, help, playfulness, support and advice have in various ways impacted upon the book and the work it describes. James Clements, Fiona Condie, Manjit Daphu, Rachel Dickinson, Kate Donelan, Noreen Faulkner, Michelle Goddard, Maria Kafkaridou, Sam Lawrenson, Carole Lee, Femi Mohammed, Jonothan Neelands, Eleanor Nesbitt, Peter O'Connor, John O'Toole, Mary Pereira, Triona Stokes, Miles Tandy, Jo Trowsdale, Dr Wing, Jackie Wrigley.

I am especially grateful to Kate Donelan, Eleanor Nesbitt, Peter O'Connor and Miles Tandy for reading draft chapters and for offering me their robust, constructive and helpful criticism.

Sections of Chapter 2 first appeared in the journal of the National Association for the Teaching of English, *English Drama Media*, in February 2004, and are published here by agreement with the journal.

Sections of Chapter 7 first appeared in *NJ* (Drama Australia Journal) vol. 27 no. 2, in October 2003 and are published here by agreement with the journal.

Finally, I would like to thank my wife, Gill, and my children, Matthew and Sally-Anne, for their support and above all their patience during the long hours of writing.

Good classroom dramas

This chapter will argue for a vision of what constitutes good drama in a primary and middle school classroom. By 'good' I mean drama that is educationally of value in itself, in human and cultural terms that include but go beyond closely defined learning objectives. Rather than referring to curriculum guidance, national frameworks or preferred outcomes it centres around something more permanent: children – what they like and what engages them, what culturally enriches and socially nourishes them.

Metaphors for drama

In my experience, primary teachers and head teachers are generally delighted to have a student who is willing to teach drama during a school placement. Not only is she welcomed as someone able to do a class assembly and help with the school production, but she is often seen as the ideal person for the annual topic on bullying with the children in the top year. Drama is often seen as *the* subject to tackle such social issues and it is, indeed, a very good vehicle for exploring them. Many Theatre in Education companies do excellent work in these areas, as do a growing number of specialists in applied drama who work outside schools with young offenders or people undergoing drug rehabilitation. However, there are dangers of drama being too readily associated with work on bullying, drug education, teenage pregnancy and the like. Such issues are rooted in the immediate social world most readily dramatised these days in soaps, and although many children enjoy soaps, they are only one of the many forms of drama, just as the ballad is only one form of poetry. Their over-emphasis can therefore limit children's drama experience. More insidiously, it can exaggerate the negative aspects of their lives, with drama being seen as a kind of medicine to tackle their social ills. The problem here lies in the metaphor. We don't enjoy taking medicine unless we are morbidly obsessed by our illnesses; we don't need it regularly, just when we are ill or sickening, when we are feeling needy rather than competent.

I therefore propose two different metaphors to help us view the potential contribution of drama to children's education and social health in a more positive light. First, drama as food. Food is enjoyable and we all need the right kind of it at regular intervals in order to grow, flourish and remain healthy. Furthermore, meals themselves can be enjoyable social occasions where we enjoy our food and the company we are in. As with a good meal, so with a good drama. The promotion of social health should go hand in hand with enjoyment, but enjoyment should be our primary purpose.

The second metaphor is one I have heard used by the acclaimed children's playwright Mike Kenny – that drama is a form of social dreaming. When we dream, the strictures of our daily experience are loosened and re-formed to create surprising and striking narratives, which experts tell us are necessary for our mental health. And the way we use the word 'dreams' to equate with our aspirations and wishes provides a further positive nuance to the concept of dreaming. For the aboriginal peoples of Australia, of course, the dreamtime is a spiritual time when the ancestors walked upon and created the land as it is and should remain. What all these meanings of dreaming carry in common is the significance of their displacement from the everyday, the immediate, the here and now. It is a time for other possibilities, other realities to be experienced and valued. The metaphor of drama time as dreamtime for primary children is not a sanction for meaningless escapism but proposes a necessary space within the incessant pressures of institutionalised schooling for children, so as to dwell in alternative narratives that can reflect their desires and aspirations.

Good drama: an example

The drama below is the introductory lesson in a drama and English scheme based on the stories of Tom Thumb. It is one I have taught many times to children between the ages of 7 and 9 and have used with teachers and student teachers. It has always proved to be a highly successful lesson so it may be useful to examine it in the light of some principles which I believe to be at the heart of good drama with children of the primary age.

Lesson

THE ADVENTURES OF TOM THUMB – LESSON 1

Resources needed: a stick/staff; a small bottle/phial; a finger puppet of Tom Thumb.

1. Ask children to move through space and when you say 'Freeze!' to make themselves as small as they can. Do this three times, asking them to make themselves even smaller each time.

2. Ask 'How small were you – as small as a . . . ?' Listen to some answers then tell children that the drama is about someone very small indeed and begins long ago with an old lady who longed for a child. Move the children into a circle and place a chair at its centre.

3. Explain to the children that you need two of them to step into the circle to take on the role of two characters. They will only need to mime what you narrate and repeat any speech you provide for them. Sit one child on the chair and give the other your staff, then begin the narration.

> *Once upon a time, long, long ago, the famous wizard Merlin was walking through a wood on a cold winter's day when he came to an old cottage. There he stopped because he could hear the voice of an old woman, humming a sad song (hum it and have all the children echo it). Then he heard her speak. 'Oh how sad and lonely I am. All my life I have wanted a little child, a son and now I am too old. A little boy would make me so happy, a baby I could tickle with my thumb . . .' (back into the song). Merlin stopped and asked for some food. The woman searched her shelves, then searched her cupboards. All she found was an old crust of bread and a thimble full of water which she offered to him. Merlin thanked the woman, took each in turn, ate and drank and waved goodbye.*

> Note: the narration needs to emphasise very clear actions.

4. The two children go back into the circle. Narrate: *Moved by her words and her generosity Merlin resolved to help her. Back in his cave, he found all his helpers.* Then, in role as Merlin, carrying the staff to signal your role, speak to the children. *'Ahh there you are. Now, there's something very important you can do to help me . . .'* Select volunteers to help you make the spell that will give the old lady the son she wants. Send a child to collect your spell book, others to collect your cauldron, ladle, water from the well, etc. All of this, of course, is mimed, and children can use their bodies to form the cauldron, bookstand, fire, etc. Ask other helpers to gather the herbs you ask for as you read the recipe, then to put them into the cauldron and stir them in. Involve the children in selecting what should go into the cauldron by pretending that you have lost your glasses and are unable to read the spell properly. *'It says I need ten stinging. . . . Oh, can you tell me what the next word says?'* Further play can include tasting the potion, spitting it out, adding sugar, etc. When it is finally ready, have a child ladle some into the phial and then have all of the children repeat the following spell with simple actions:

> *Old woman, you will soon give birth*
> *Before the spring has come*

To a wonder-child, a tiny boy
No bigger than your thumb.

Admit that the potion will only work if the person who takes it doesn't know what it is for. Ask for two volunteers and rehearse with them, with the other children's help, what they need to say to convince the old lady to drink it.

5. Play a game of **Huggy** to put children into threes. Two of them are to be the helpers, the other the old lady. Can she be persuaded to take the potion?

6. Back in role as Merlin, bring the children into the circle again, question and congratulate them on how they got on with the old woman. Then admit that you are pleased but still a little puzzled. *'A strange request, I know, but it is what she wanted, a child no bigger than her thumb, she said. I wonder why??'* Prompt the children to realise Merlin's mistake and to help him realise it, too. They need to explain how he misheard her. Once they have done this, become flustered and worried. The old lady must be told! Ask the children to talk in small groups to see if they can come up with any ideas to convince her that it might be a good thing after all to have a child that small (e.g. cheap on clothes, food, possessions, easy to carry around, etc.). Pool these ideas together and list at least five.

7. Ask for two volunteers who will return to see the old lady, and with the class's help coach them in what they will be saying to her. Then take on the role of the old woman yourself and make it difficult for them! Narrate: *As the two helpers approached the cottage, the old lady greeted them warmly.* You can't wait for your son who will soon be tall and strong and will help you with all of your heavy chores! Allow children in the circle to advise the two volunteers on things they can say to prepare the old lady gently for the truth. When they finally tell you how small the baby will be, listen to the arguments they have prepared and conclude by saying that you would rather have him tiny than not at all; and that you will love him whether he is big, small, fat, thin, well-behaved or naughty . . .

8. . . . which is just as well, because, when Tom Thumb was born, he did turn out to be quite a naughty boy!!

Ask the children to get into space. They are to mime the following actions in their own space as you narrate them (it's best if you mime with them):

Tom Thumb wasn't like an ordinary baby. He was a fully grown little boy in four days! He was hardly ever tired, so, when his mother sent him to bed, he crawled through the crack underneath the door and ran to the top of the stairs and looked down. Whoah! It was a very long way down!

Using a belt from his mother's dressing gown, he made a loop, swung it around his head and caught it around the top of the banister. He climbed up like a mountaineer. Once at the top he got ready and then wheeee! He slid the whole of the way down the banister like an olympic skier before landing with a bump!!! Ooh! Dusting himself off he got up and looked around him when a lovely smell came to his nose. Mmmmm! It smelt like his favourite pudding which was . . . (use a child's suggestion). Tom followed the smell into the dining room and stopped at the base of what for him was a huge table. How was he going to get up there? (Use children's ideas.) Once on the table he tried to jump up into the dish but it was too high. How was he going to get into it?? (use children's ideas, if you like . . . or . . .) . . . so he hauled up the dessert spoon and dropped it on to the side of the dish to make a ramp. Up, up, up he walked, taking care not to lose his balance. Yummy!!! As he looked into the dish, Tom saw a big piece of pudding floating on the top of the custard (cream/sauce). One, two, three, he jumped on to it and began to paddle over to the pudding and, climbing on to it, he began to eat huge mouthfuls. Imagine! A whole island made of pudding! Heaven! But, oh no, who was this coming up to the table?? Yes, Tom's mum! Quickly, he took a deep breath and dived under the custard. But she took a spoonful and Tom was in it and saw himself getting closer to his mum's mouth so he began to jump up and down on the spoon shouting 'Mum! Don't eat me! Don't eat me!!' Imagine his mother's shock when she saw Tom! With a scream, she threw the spoon up in the air and away Tom flew higher and higher until he started to fall back down towards the table. As he fell he saw a jug of water beneath him so he steered for it and dived into it with a great big splash and up he swam to the surface . . . ''Cor, that was close, wasn't it mum! Mum!??'

9. How do you think his mum felt? What do you think she did to punish him? Let children share ideas. Unfortunately he was always getting up to naughty tricks – maybe next week you can think of some and write little stories about them. And maybe you can make your own Tom Thumb . . .!

10. You can introduce the finger puppet (or thumb puppet!) now and answer the children's questions as they 'hot thumb' him for a minute or two. Be friendly but a bit cheeky in your responses.

Follow-up

Possible follow-up classroom activities:

- Children write up the story of how Tom Thumb was nearly eaten by his own mother based upon Activity 8.
- Make a Tom Thumb corner by asking children to look out for different things that his mum could have used for his clothes, his bed, a hat, a bath, etc.

- Children discuss various places Tom might go – to school, for example, or to the shops with his mum. Because he is so small, what kind of naughty things might he get up to in these places? Children write their own stories around a simple structure.
- Children in groups write a short list, e.g. *For his hat he wore an acorn cup /For his bath he used a shell/For his trampoline he used a spider's web*, etc. These can be enriched with adjectives and turned into short poems, e.g. *For his trampoline he used a silky, springy spider's web*, etc.
- Read or tell episodes from the original Tom Thumb story.[1]
- Make thumb puppets.
- Tell children that the queen of the fairies gave Tom a present of a magic ring and a magic hat. These had special powers. Discuss with the children what these might have been and work their suggestions into later drama work.

Good drama is a bit like magic

There is nothing magical about good drama teaching. As with any pedagogy, it is skilful, a craft, and can be learned. But drama itself has a quality of magic to it.

Magic is the power that changes someone or something into someone or something else; that makes things appear or disappear; that turns the ordinary into something extraordinary. Stories of magic fascinate adults as well as children, as the phenomenon of *Harry Potter* has underlined. In drama children can not only act out stories with a magical content but they also engage in an imaginative act that in many ways reflects the transformative powers of magic. The space we are in we imagine as another space; the people we are we imagine as other people; we see objects where there are no objects, sea where there is only blue cloth, a magic potion where there is only a bottle. Time is elastic. We can travel forwards or backwards in it, make it move quickly or slowly, even make it stand still. Even when the stories we are enacting are firmly rooted in the 'real' social world, the form in which we experience them is, in this imaginative sense, magical.

In Tom Thumb, the story has magic at its heart, of course – a wizard, a magic spell, a boy who is impossibly small – but its success as a drama lesson will depend upon yours and the children's willingness to create the imaginary world together and upon how well you manage the transformative powers of their imaginations, just as magicians manage ours when they create their illusions. Hence the importance of activities such as the mimetic play in Activity 4 and the narrated action in Activity 8, when the teacher and class act out Tom's first adventure together. Get these right and children will have a vivid experience of the thrills and risks – and hence the imaginative appeal – of being as small as Tom Thumb.

Good drama holds the promise of a good story

Stories are perhaps the most direct link between drama and English work. My own drama work is usually inspired by a good story. When teachers ask me why I use stories so much my answer is a simple one: because a good story is a better teacher than I am. Successful drama lessons depend upon the lure of the story and the way the story is put together, or plotted. Of course, there are many different kinds of story that children like but certain very popular dramatic stories, such as are found in popular films, contain recurring features that can inform our understanding.

Heroes, heroines and monsters

Children enjoy stories of good triumphing over evil. They like their heroes and heroines to be admirable but not perfect and their monsters to be frightening and powerful but not invincible. Tom Thumb is a good example of the kind of hero that appeals to children as he reflects but also transcends their everyday experience. Like them he is small, unlike them he is powerful; like them he is punished when he is naughty, unlike them he has amazing adventures as a result. Children enjoy the fact that he is at once admirable and subversive. He is adventurous and takes risks but flouts authority. He is cheeky and will over-indulge his appetites given half a chance. But he has a keen sense of justice, particularly when he sees the weak being bullied by the strong. In the follow-up drama lesson, he ends up trapped in a short-sighted woman's purse but then helps her get the better of a bully who tries to rob her.

Teachers are often rightly anxious to challenge stereotypes and may be concerned about the stereotypical qualities of heroes and villains. Is, for example, Tom Thumb offering a particularly male version of heroism and reinforcing unhelpful behaviour patterns in boys that impede them from succeeding in school? Such questions are important and gender is one of the key points of identity through which children mark themselves out in their twin desires for similarity and difference. Similarly with villains and monsters, witches and wicked stepmothers: how far does what we portray as evil, as 'other', symbolically demonise particular social groups? These are complex and important issues that emerge at various points in the book, but for now I would simply propose that we refrain from blanket censorship and offer a balance to children over time. Our dramas and our stories need a variety of heroes and villains of both genders, collective as well as individual acts of bravery, attractive and deceptive monsters as well as grotesque ones. We also need to consider the representation in context. The old lady in the second Tom Thumb lesson at the end of this chapter is, on the surface, a stereotypical image of an old person as victim. However, in the later part of the drama, she is placed in a strong position of power to exact revenge from the robber.

If tales of heroism and villainy excite children, tales of foolishness often amuse them and can help build their self-confidence. After all, they'd never be so stupid themselves! Merlin is an interesting character for children as he is a supposedly wise person who does a foolish thing, a sympathetic adult who needs their advice to sort out a problem of his own making.

Secrets and lies

Children love secrets and know all about lies and the reasons for telling them. Drama thrives on both. Just count them in the next episode of your favourite soap! *Do you think we are being told everything? Should we trust her? Should we tell him what we know? What do you think she is keeping hidden in that bag? Who was this letter written to?* Such questions are the life-blood of interesting dramas with children. When attempting to persuade the old lady to drink the potion in Activity 4, children can be offered the challenge of finding a series of believable lies; or of not really lying at all (saying to her, 'If you drink it, your wishes will come true', for example). In Activity 7, the challenge for the children is how to let the old lady gently into the secret that her baby won't be quite what she is expecting! Children will not be lying here but they will be putting a spin on the truth. Lying when in role may not only be permissible, it may sometimes be necessary. Such moral ambiguity sometimes worries teachers, but it shouldn't. It is essentially part of the playfulness of drama and can help children sharpen their wits as well as their sense of humour. Sometimes it may be morally defensible – lying to a villain to protect a friend, for example. Reflecting upon these instances can help develop children's moral thinking.

Clues and surprises

A good drama drops clues as to how it might develop, and part of the satisfaction we get from it is in experiencing the logic of the story as the plot unfolds. Children enjoy this speculative side of drama and very young children will often make their predictions aloud. *He's going to find it now! He shouldn't have done that!* This propensity for speculation is one that teachers can readily exploit in the reflective phases of a drama lesson and it can both develop and refine children's understanding of story structure. But there is always a tension between logic and predictability. Children will enjoy a drama with a few surprises more than one that is too easy to predict. In Tom Thumb the surprise in Activity 6 is particularly satisfying as the clue has been there all along in the original words of the old lady. The further surprise for the children in Activity 7, when as the old lady the teacher in role says how much she is looking forward to having a big, strong son, presents a sudden and unprepared challenge which they enjoy because it is highly playful. After all, teachers usually help and prompt children through carefully prepared activities, they don't normally set traps for them!

Journeys and challenges

Good dramas often involve journeys of some kind – journeys of exploration, quests to find something or someone special, flights to or from danger. On these journeys there are challenges to overcome and thresholds to cross, usually guarded by gatekeepers who must be either tricked or won over. For children their appeal lies in the imaginative promise of life itself, a journey that lies ahead of them. Essentially, however, these journeys are more about self-discovery for the characters involved – from ignorance to self-knowledge, from danger to safety, from isolation to community, from dependency to independence. The sequence of drama lessons I teach on Tom Thumb symbolically traces his journey from childishness to adulthood. In the first we learn how he is born and experience his mischievousness (i.e. childishness); in the second we see how he begins to use his talent for mischief for the purposes of good; in the third we have an adventure where we help him rescue Merlin from an evil sorcerer. The scheme in Chapter 4 on 'The Selfish Giant' does not involve a physical journey, but the story is a spiritual journey for the giant himself, one of self-discovery and redemption.

Good drama is highly playful

At the heart of drama is the human spirit of playfulness. Our society has highly ambivalent attitudes towards play. On the one hand it is equated with leisure and therefore as the opposite of work; with fantasy and escapism and therefore contrary to reality; as 'not serious' and therefore not to be taken seriously; or as childish and therefore something to grow out of. Viewed from this perspective, we can begin to understand why there are powerful forces in our culture that undervalue and mistrust play within the context of schools, particularly when these same forces see the primary purpose of education as an economic one, to prepare children for adult work in the real world. In the UK we have a National Curriculum that enshrines the view that play should make way for work when children reach the age of 5. Yet it is easy to point out some major contradictions within this binary outlook that is held by our culture towards work and play. Take football, for instance. The verb is to 'play' football, but would anyone deny the fact that there is hard, physical work involved in being a professional footballer? Or that people take it very seriously indeed? And paradoxically, those people who 'play' for a living, such as actors, sportsmen and women and musicians, can receive not only great adulation but vast amounts of income, too. This is only possible because our culture also celebrates and greatly values play at the same time as it seems to decry its worth in schools.

Playfulness, then, is a deeply human quality, pervasive through our culture. It is something we enjoy and should openly value, and children's propensity to enjoy play is used to energise the Tom Thumb lesson. Driving it all is their willingness to pretend that they are elsewhere and other than they are. Allied to this is the sense of challenge that is inherent to play, both physical and verbal – can they make themselves smaller? Can they make their bodies look like a cauldron? Can they talk the old lady round? Note that it is the challenge, not the easiness, that children enjoy here. Once, in a drama with a class of eight- and nine-year-olds, the children were in role as a group of escaping slaves. I asked if they wanted me to make their escape easy or hard. 'Hard!' came the unanimously loud chorus – led, incidentally, by the girls. But crucial to the whole mix is the teacher's willingness to play, too – not only that, but to play harder than the children themselves. Only then will children believe that you value drama yourself, and in this way your own play can become a licence and a model for theirs. When a child brings me an imaginary ladle (Activity 4), I'll usually send them back and tell them to bring me the large silver one next to it. When the old lady is searching for some food (Activity 3), I'll make her stretch up to the highest shelf in the cupboard and search it carefully before declaring that there was nothing there, only some dust that made her sneeze.

How we play with children will of course vary with their age. For example, when I have just been hot-seated as a character by children under 7, I will often, in re-adopting my role as teacher, speak as if I had been out of the classroom at the time. *Did you meet the wolf then? Really!! Was he nice? No?! Why, what did he say to you?* Children enjoy this playful interaction. They enjoy its humorous edge but it also sends a clear signal that their teacher takes playfulness very seriously. With older children I often emphasise the game element of hot-seating by taking on the role of a character who is coolly and calmly lying to them and implicitly daring them to catch me out. This kind of playfulness is serious without being solemn and sanctions the idea that we can learn and laugh at one and the same time.

Of course, there is another reason why children enjoy these particular examples of playfulness on the part of the teacher; they are a bit naughty. I am playing little tricks on them, which they accept because there is nothing malicious or personalised in them. The children involved are included in the laughter and are not the butt of any kind of practical joke. These tricks are not really tricks; they are playful challenges, illustrative of the kind of playfulness that characterises much improvised drama, from *commedia dell'arte* to TV shows such as *Whose Line Is It Anyway?*

Naughtiness is a key element in what can make drama attractive to children. The Tom Thumb drama has a naughty but good-hearted child at its centre, and just how naughty he can be is the subject of two of the listed follow-up activities. I will return to this important aspect of drama towards the end of this chapter, as it carries its risks as well as its rewards for teachers. Suffice it to say for the time being that going to a drama lesson should be nothing like going to church; a sense of playful naughtiness will guarantee you more successful drama lessons than pious moralising ever will.

Good dramas need to be well-structured

Structure is key to the success of a drama lesson in ways that go beyond the structure of the story itself. Dorothy Heathcote has remarked upon three simple tensions that can help us understand the dynamics of dramatic structure: movement and stillness; sound and silence; light and dark.[2] Because drama is essentially physical, the physical rhythm of the activities needs to be carefully considered. Are children being asked to sit in a circle for too long? Are they being given sufficient time for reflection? In addition, we need to plan a good balance between teacher-led and independent dramatic play; between activities which demand quiet (the careful ladling of the magic potion into the phial in Activity 4, for example) and those where the whole class is vocal, as in the chanting of the spell moments later, or the group work in Activity 5. As for light and dark, it is perhaps more useful for a primary teacher to consider this in terms of atmosphere rather than the physical use of light, although simply turning off the classroom lights can be very effective in generating tension. Does the drama have moments of light-heartedness as well as seriousness, humour as well as sadness? Tom Thumb is essentially a comic drama but there are moments of poignancy, such as the old woman's lament in Activity 3 and her eventual testimony that she will love her child whatever he turns out to be like in Activity 7. There are also dark elements in the humour, such as when Tom nearly gets eaten by his mother! Striving for a balance and a rhythm to our drama lessons is part and parcel of securing the children's continuing interest and concentration.

Another tension for the teacher to consider is the balance between her agenda, or sense of direction for the lesson, and those moments where the children themselves can influence what happens. This is what Neelands has called the balance between 'necessary constraint and necessary freedom'.[3] My own approach here is to imagine the lesson as an excursion through a wood, where the teacher's duty is to know the terrain well and make sure that everyone stays together, goes in the same direction and gets to the planned destination more or less at the same time. However, because this excursion is across interesting terrain, there are many points along the way where we will stop to explore. Here children will be told what they might look for and where they are allowed to explore before coming back into the group. I imagine this space as a large playground with a fence around it. Then, depending upon what we have found, I will choose which path I think we should take in order to proceed to the next playground on our route.

Good dramas are emotionally charged

When it works well, drama carries an emotional charge that holds children in its power. At different moments they might be intrigued, moved, amused, outraged, excited, tense, elated. What we don't want them to be is bored. These emotions are inextricably linked to their understanding of what is happening, and the extent of their emotional engagement will depend upon how much they care about the people in the story. In other words, values are central to drama, and that is why it is such a good vehicle to help children explore them. Questions like *Why do you think Merlin wanted to help the old lady?* will encourage them to consider their own understanding of pity and generosity and compare it to the understandings of others. Asking your class *Who thinks Tom deserves to be punished by his mum? Why/why not?* can open up a discussion about what they consider to be naughty behaviour and fair punishment. A question such as *Why do you think the old lady wanted a baby so much?* will encourage them to articulate their understandings of loneliness and of the different reasons why grown-ups might want to have children. Of course, different children will have different answers to these questions, which is rather the point of asking them in the first place. They will draw their answers from their own experiences but, as drama is a communal art form, their understandings will immediately enter a shared arena and become a class resource for considering issues of value together, both now and in the future.

Good drama is liberating

Through imaginative engagement in drama, various tyrannies that govern our everyday actions are loosened, in particular the tyranny of identity. For the teacher, this means that you can be freed from always having to talk and act as teacher. Instead, you can talk and act as a kind old wizard, a lonely old woman or as a cheeky child. For children, the freedom is more potent. Instead of being powerless, they can take on the role of someone powerful. Instead of performing a social role that they may well not be happy with – a child deemed to have special needs, for example – they can become someone who is respected and listened to. For some children this can have immediate and notable results. Most teachers who have experience of drama can tell stories of children who were quiet, of low self-esteem or identified as needy in some way, who suddenly gained a voice in drama time.

This loosening of tyrannies is not risk-free for the teacher, however, as another loosening occurs at the boundaries that mark out what constitutes permissible behaviour from what does not. With some classes the moral code of the classroom can suddenly appear to be under threat as certain individuals begin to transgress those boundaries to see how far they can push them. Essentially what these children are doing is attempting to renegotiate codes of behaviour that are no longer as clear as they were. Hence some form of contracting between teacher and children is essential and some tips to assist those of you inexperienced in drama are included in Appendix 2. Although such a contract is necessary, your class should not feel as if they are being tightly controlled, as they are in the literacy hour, for example. A key aim is for you all to come out at the end of the lesson feeling good, having experienced the exhilaration of a special kind of imaginative freedom that is integral to the enjoyment of drama. That is why many of the best ways to control a drama lesson lie within the logic of the story itself. We need silence or the spell won't work; we need to speak one at a time or Merlin won't be able to hear your advice. My advice is, on the whole, to trust children's desire and ability to play, to trust the appeal of a good story and to use only those controls that are necessary.

To conclude this chapter we return to the drama of Tom Thumb. It is fashionable in some books for the author to set tasks at the end of the chapter for you to reflect upon and apply the theory you have just read. I would like to make that highly practical. If you decide to teach the Tom Thumb lessons, then it may well be worth your while looking at the following plan and seeing whether the principles I have been proposing can be seen in practice; and reflecting upon what you can do to apply them yourself in your own teaching.

Lesson

THE ADVENTURES OF TOM THUMB – LESSON 2

1. Put the children into threes and have them sit down in space. Explain to them that today we will learn how Tom managed to earn his magic hat and ring. Begin by modelling Tom in his room – naughty again! – looking out of his attic window. Describe what he sees – the roof, gutter, a tree, leaves blowing about in the wind, birds flying . . . 'How can I escape?' he wonders. Ask the children to work out a way and then to show it in their groups as a **still image**, adding a caption to the picture to describe it.

2. Still in threes, tell the children that within a few seconds of escaping, Tom ended up inside the purse of a short-sighted old lady. As with the previous exercise, children form an image to illustrate it and add a caption to it. The image can contain some movement if children find it helpful.

    Note: the problem of the difference in scale here is one that children won't worry about. The fact that they are in threes can help – e.g. one child might be the purse!

3. Children now work individually in space. Ask them to copy you as you narrate. *Meanwhile a robber was approaching . . .* Stand then walk like him together. *He saw a little child's ball – 'I'll stamp on that and burst it!' he said.* Get individual children to demonstrate how he stamped on it, how he laughed and then all copy together.

4. Then bring children into a circle and tell them to watch what happened next. Perform a brief dialogue between the old lady and the robber to demonstrate how he steals her purse, modelling the physical and vocal characteristics of each.

> *'Hey, old woman, give me your purse.'*
> *'But it has all my money in it!'*
> *'Exactly! Give it to me!'*
> *'But then I'll have nothing to eat!'*
> *'I don't care!'*
> *And with that the robber snatched the purse, placed it in his back pocket, laughed and walked off.*

5. Still in the circle, ask the children where Tom Thumb was when all this was happening. And did he hear what happened, I wonder? Put on the thumb puppet and talk to the children as Tom Thumb. *'What can I do? Is there anything in this purse to help?'* It will help if you have, say, a couple of yellow hoops on hand as coins and – very important – a cane as a needle! *'Coins . . . ow! What's this? Well here's a big sharp needle – what can I do with this??'* Children should quickly have ideas of exactly what you can do with it! *'You mean I should stick this in the robber's . . . ?? Can you show me?'* As a child demonstrates three or four times, he effectively takes on the role of Tom. Get the whole class to their feet to jump and scream each time the child thrusts the pin into the imaginary bottom (the more vicious the thrust the better!)

6. Ask children to sit again and resume the narration, how the robber jumped and screamed until he finally took out the purse and spoke to it. *'You must be a magic purse! Why are you causing me such pain?'* And Tom had an idea – *'I'm going to make this robber return the purse and make sure he changes his ways!'* Using the thumb puppet, ask the children what you should say to him?' Repeat what the children suggest via the thumb puppet then, as the robber, holding and looking down at the purse, reply and ask *'And if I do that will you stop hurting me?'* The children can now suggest a series of tasks that the robber must do to make amends to the old lady for his crime. The robber will agree to each of

them in turn, becoming increasingly desperate, each time asking if that is all he need do.

7. In pairs, the children now act out the robber returning the purse to the old lady and doing the things for her that the children have suggested. Encourage whichever child is taking on the role of the old lady to make him do more things for her if she can think of any.

8. Then tell the children how, after the robber had left, Tom popped out of the purse and told the old lady what he had done. She was delighted and wanted to kiss him but Tom thought *uuuurggghhh* and ran off to find Merlin's helpers. As Tom, ask, *'Do you think I did well? Do you think Merlin will be pleased with me?'*

9. Now Merlin wanted to check this story out in his crystal ball to see if it was really as Tom had said – he could be such a liar! – but, sure enough, he saw the pictures that confirmed Tom's story. Negotiate with the children what these were through a series of picture titles, e.g.
   - Tom escapes from his bedroom
   - Tom ends up in the lady's purse
   - The old lady is robbed
   - Tom sticks a pin into the robber
   - Tom talks to the robber from the purse
   - The robber returns the purse to the woman
   - The robber makes amends for his crime

10. These captions can be shared out among the children to work on in their literacy groups. The task for the class is to produce a written and illustrated version of the story as it appeared in the crystal ball, with each group being responsible for one or two images and the accompanying text. This should be a carefully drafted and redrafted piece of work. Using digital photography, text boxes and sound files, the completed story can then be shown as a powerpoint display.

Notes

1 See pp. 154–167 in Kevin Crossley-Holland's *British Folk Tales*, London, Orchard Books, 1987.

2 D. Heathcote, 'Signs and Portents', in E. Johnson and C. O'Neill (eds), *Dorothy Heathcote: Collected Writings on Education and Drama*, London, Hutchinson, 1984.

3 J. Neelands, 'The Space in Our Hearts', *Journal of National Drama*, Summer 2002.

CHAPTER 2

Drama and English

An integrated approach

Drama and a social theory of language

'Matthew, pick that up, please. Now you know where it should go, don't you? Well done!'

Change the child's name and these three simple sentences could have been spoken by any number of primary teachers or student teachers in any number of classrooms. And yet a brief analysis of them can tell us a lot about the social function of language and what drama can contribute to children's language learning. As they stand, these sentences will probably make immediate sense to you. You can imagine a variety of objects the teacher might be referring to – the child's lunchbox, a screwed up crisp packet, a paint brush – all of which would have specific places were they to belong in your own classroom. It is your familiarity with the *context* – the primary classroom – that enables you to begin to read meanings into these words.

On the surface, the *purpose* of the teacher's words may appear to be clear and simple enough – to get Matthew to put something away. But how do you imagine Matthew? How old is he? Is English his first language? Is he responsible for making a mess or is the teacher just asking for his assistance? Does he really know where 'it' should go or has he forgotten? To understand this we need more information, not only about Matthew, his previous and current actions and the object he is picking up, but also about the teacher herself. All of this we could see or infer better if we were to witness these words being spoken. Is the teacher cross with Matthew? In which case there could well be a sharpness to her tone and a note of irony in her 'Well done!' intended to inform Matthew and the class that untidiness annoys her. Is he always making a mess? In which case there might be a resigned note of patience in her voice which hints to the class that her patience won't last forever.

The teacher won't just be using words and tone of voice to send these messages out to Matthew and the class. Hands on hips accompanied by a frown may well signal that she is getting cross, whereas arms folded, a sag of the shoulders and a slight raising of the eyebrows with a brief but noticeable glance in the direction of the waste paper bin might clearly signal the fragility of her patience.

Now what if I were to tell you that these words were, in fact, spoken by a student teacher in the first week of a new school placement? We can see immediately that they could well be communicating a lot more than a request to a particular boy to tidy something away. They could be part of a self-conscious performance as she tries out her new role as teacher. In order to be seen as a 'real' teacher she must prove herself able to communicate not only information to children but also her own authority. Tone of voice, facial expression, body language, she needs to get these right if the children are to accept her as their teacher, as someone who spends her time telling them what to do all day.

We all of us have to play different social roles in our daily lives, and these roles require us to use different language codes, both physical and spoken. Because of this, we need to know when to switch from one code to another. If our student teacher were to become so engrossed with her role as teacher that she repeated these words in the same tenor that evening to Matthew the barman when he dropped a five pound note, she might be more than a little embarrassed by his response. How I use and perform language as a teacher differs from how I use and perform it as a customer in a grocer's shop, as a friend drinking socially in a bar, or as a professional colleague in a staff meeting.

There is still an additional layer of paralinguistic complexity to this speech act, of particular importance to our student teacher. Let us suppose that she was being observed by her university supervisor at the time and that he was unimpressed by a perceived sharpness, even sarcasm, in her tone, something he makes clear in his feedback notes. She feels that this comment is unfair, that she was being neither sharp nor sarcastic, just firm; and that she was simply following advice given to her on a previous placement, that she should emulate the class teacher's own style. On making her feelings known to the class teacher, she is given strong support. The issue here is clearly one of interpretation but also of values. Language, how we use it and understand it, is saturated with values, and these are enmeshed within issues of social and cultural power. What is at stake for the different characters in this example is as much about whose perceptions will be given most credence when the student's teaching is assessed as it is about which of them is right or not. This becomes particularly acute if we consider issues of gender and ethnicity. Let us suppose, for example, that the supervisor is a white male and the student a black female. Do we have the same perception of the disagreement if the supervisor and Matthew were both black males and the student a white female?

From the above analysis of these three short sentences we can draw the following important conclusions, of particular relevance to language learning:

1. To make sense of language, whether speech or print on a page, we must have a clear idea of the context within which it is embedded and the purpose for which it is intended.

2. Making sense of the purpose of a speech act goes beyond an ability to decipher or recognize the literal meaning of the actual words used. It depends upon an appreciation of particular human intentions and relationships, many of which are expressed 'beneath' the text, i.e. as subtext.

3. Spoken language is embodied, and much of what we communicate comes from the visual and aural signals – facial expression, gesture, tone of voice – that accompany our words.

4. In order to be effective as social beings, we must be able to select and perform language appropriately in the variety of roles we play in our daily lives.

5. Much in language use is indeterminate, not fixed or transparent. We actively make sense of language rather than passively absorb it.

6. Issues of social and cultural value permeate the meanings we construct from and with language.

These statements effectively constitute an argument for a social theory of language. If we accept their validity, then it follows that drama, the most social of art forms, has a key contribution to make to children's language learning. The reasons for this are listed below, illustrated with examples drawn from work with both lower and upper primary children to be found later in this book:

1. Drama, more than any other subject in the curriculum, mirrors life as it is lived and experienced. In a written story, context is defined through words alone. In drama, however, it is actually constructed from space, objects and people as well as words. Language can therefore be experienced – heard, interpreted and used – in contexts that seem real to children. Because of the concrete and physical nature of the experience, the purposes of the language use are more immediate and accessible to them.

   EXAMPLES: Children take on the roles of workers in the imaginative play area set up as a garden centre. They read a letter from the giant, prepare themselves for his visit and then advise him in person as to what he needs for his garden. (4:4i)

   Children examine and discuss objects in Caliban's cave, including a message in a bottle. They then help physically to 'create' Caliban before meeting and hot-seating him. (5:2c)

2. In drama, strong contexts make children actively aware of subtexts, or meanings beneath the surface of words.

EXAMPLES: A certain Mr Smith makes an appearance, enquiring after a missing child. The children in role as servants recognise him from a description the child has given them. They know immediately that, whatever Mr Smith says, he is not to be trusted. (3:3d)

Children consider and physicalise the emotions that they feel underlie the words of the villagers as they speak to Shanga. (6:1d)

3. In drama, children are encouraged both to read and convey meaning through embodied language.

    EXAMPLES: Children create the barriers with their bodies and vocalise the signs that are meant to keep trespassers out of the giant's garden (4:2a, b)

    Children embody the words of the villagers in physicalised group tableaux. (6:1d)

4. Drama can be used to present children with opportunities both to use language and to analyse its use in a variety of social roles.

    EXAMPLES: Children need to persuade Sir Roger, a politician, to help two political refugees. (3:5b)

    Children in pairs take on the roles of Prospero, Ferdinand, Caliban or Miranda to create, perform and discuss short scenes that illustrate the relationships between this particular father and daughter, master and slave, etc. (5:3c)

5. In drama children can be encouraged to explore ambiguity rather than find a single answer; and to play with the richness and suggestiveness of language rather than always to regard its meanings as transparent.

    EXAMPLES: Children suggest and play with a variety of words to describe the giant at different points in the story so far. They organise these into short poems. (4:3d)

    Children play expressively with words from the text of *Blodin the Beast*. (6:4b)

6. Drama can provide a space for children to articulate different interpretations of language events and to explore the values that permeate them.

    EXAMPLES: Children speculate upon why the giant is so grumpy and ungrateful. (4:1h)

    Children are asked to reconsider the symbolic meaning of Blodin the Beast and their possible complicity in his monstrousness. (6:5b, c)

How drama enriches English and literacy learning

Much teaching of English in the primary classroom, particularly in recent years, has concentrated on the skills of literacy, on enabling children to read and write. As a result, the UK's National Literacy Strategy, for all its complexity, tends to favour the secretarial or technical skills of language. Of course, these are highly important, but the underlying philosophy emphasises language as a body of skills to be mastered and deployed. As a result, many language exercises become divorced from context, as it is the skill rather than the experience that is seen as important. I have, for example, seen children taught how to write the instructions for constructing a model aircraft without ever seeing one, let alone making one. The context here is narrowly self-referential – how to learn a skill rather than how to do anything purposeful with it. With this view of learning, even speaking and listening become similarly self-referential, as though their chief purpose was to support reading and writing. Good drama creates vividly imagined, fictional contexts which can make language activities, including those which are skills-based, seem not only purposeful but even fun and exciting to children. It also puts speaking and listening at the heart of language learning – as it still is in the social and economic world, despite the relentless march of email and the internet!

The literacy hour, for all its skilful pedagogy, depends upon one social register, that of teacher–pupil exchange, ordinarily of the question–answer model, with the teacher knowing the answer to the question in advance. This type of talk is dominant in the classroom and yet is untypical of other social situations. Classroom discussion tends to be restricted within tightly boundaried topics, again with few potential avenues for manoeuvre, as skills-based learning objectives are necessarily specific and clearly delineated. Drama by its very nature can complement this narrowness of spoken register and learning objectives. In the fictional worlds it creates, children can be the experts rather than the teacher; they can frame and ask the questions; they can playfully practise the registers of authority. Closely allied with this is the nature of the important learning objectives in drama, which often tend to be what Eliot Eisner called 'expressive' rather than 'instructional', focusing on those open-ended aspects of learning, where we enrich our knowledge by exploring concepts through talk and action to complement our learning of skills.[1]

Within the framework of the National Literacy Strategy, as in all kinds of instructional teaching, teachers tend to strive for transparency not only in their language, but also in their intended learning outcomes. What children are supposed to learn needs to be clear, and it needs to be clear whether they have learned it or not. This approach to teaching works very well for skills but not so well for other important areas of learning, such as the indeterminate area of social and moral concepts. It's easy to tell whether I can spell the word 'justice' or not, and I can even be tested on its dictionary definition. It is, however, far more difficult to know whether I appreciate its significance in social affairs, let alone whether I can be expected to apply it or even recognize it in my own social dealings. Here we need to find ways of engaging children with ideas, some of which can be quite abstract in nature, and be more patient, long-term and open-ended in our expectations. As adults, we can discuss moral issues such as justice, self-sacrifice and deceitfulness quite readily, drawing upon a wealth of knowledge and experience to illustrate what we have to say. Children not only have more limited experiences, they also find abstract language far more alien to their own daily usage. This is one reason why good stories are educationally so important, as they can help children discuss and engage with complex moral and social issues through the use of more concrete rather than abstract language.

The particular contribution of drama to such talk, intended to develop children's ability to use language to explore subtle and ambivalent human issues, is threefold. First of all, the imaginative experience of fiction through drama is more immediate than through a written story. Children feel they have lived through or have actually witnessed the experience. As a result, their talk can be situated *within* the experience as well as being *reflective of* the experience under discussion. Second, because the language of drama is more sensorial than mere words, making use of visual and other aural signals, it offers more of what we might call 'avenues of engagement' for children to access the human issues within a story. Some children may read a facial expression or a physical gesture more readily than they understand printed or spoken words. Third, drama does not spell things out as clearly as a written text does, since the narrative commentary, which often provides access to a character's inner life, is generally absent. Instead of reading about Prospero's motives and whether they were justified or not, we have to work them out by listening, watching and inferring from what he says and does. Similarly, if one group of children rehearse and act out what they feel would be a fair ending to a particular story, the resulting talk is anchored to physical representation but dependent upon interpretation. We can say, therefore, that a dramatic text is a more open text than a straightforward written narrative as there is more scope for different interpretations or different nuances of interpretation. This openness can be instrumental in enriching classroom discussion.

Most of the argument in this chapter so far has centred around the central importance of speaking and listening in children's language learning and drama's role within this. Many people, teachers among them, will still see reading and writing as the key preoccupations of English teaching. However, recent changes of emphasis within national literacy training have refocused strongly upon speaking and listening, or oracy, and it is now widely accepted that improvements in reading and writing are intrinsically related to improvements in oracy. The second half of this chapter will look closely at purposeful ways in which reading and writing can be integrated into drama activities and will examine examples of children's work and what teachers had to say about it.

In seeing reading and writing as fundamental to, but not the only important aspect of literacy, we are, in fact, recognizing and responding to key cultural and economic developments that are happening on a global scale. Visual literacy – the ability to read, critically interpret and manipulate visual messages – is increasingly important to us all. Stories, both factual and fictitious, are told and witnessed more and more on TV, video, DVD and cinema screens than in print. The internet provides us with information in both visual and printed form, the one complementing the other. As a result, the ability to understand how visual and aural languages are manipulated for particular ends is increasingly important for our democratic future. More and more, as our young people grow, they will need to relate to and communicate with people from cultural backgrounds different from their own. These contacts will increasingly permeate their political, economic and social lives. Global images from other cultures, embodying different cultural traditions, saturate our news screens and presses, and are often used to demonise particular groups. The image of an Islamic fundamentalist is easily blurred into that of an international terrorist unless we develop a critical eye as we read newspapers and watch the TV. Hence the concepts of *critical literacy* and *multiliteracies* are becoming increasingly influential globally in educational thinking. Recognizing the need for children to become multi-literate in today's world re-emphasises the importance of drama and other curriculum subjects where visual communication and issues of cultural value and social critique have always been of central concern.

Drama and reading

You may feel that the most immediate and conventional relationship between drama and reading takes the form of the play script. However, simply having children sit in groups, sharing the parts out and reading play scripts is a very limited form of drama, if it can be called drama at all. The complementary benefits that drama brings to English work, as argued in this chapter, will only be gained if children work towards bringing these scripts to life. Figure 2.1 presents a model for building such an approach to script work into the structure of the literacy hour. However, such self-contained exercises can be complemented by making reading an integral part of projects in which drama takes a central role. For the rest of this section we will examine how this can be done. The key point that needs to be made at this stage, however, is that, for it to be truly effective, reading must perform a dramatic function and not simply be an added-on exercise. It must contribute in some concrete and purposeful way to the developing drama work.

PLAY SCRIPTS IN THE LITERACY HOUR. EXAMPLE: YEAR 3, TERM 1

Have an imaginative play area set up in part of the classroom and refer to it as the performance area.

WHOLE CLASS INTRO (15 MINS)

Shared work on sections of play script drawing attention to *different* elements each day. Focus your attention on one or two of the following per day:

- Technical aspects – dialogue, layout, stage directions.
- Interpretive aspects – how does the character feel now, do you think? How might they say this line? Would they shout or whisper it? Will a volunteer demonstrate for us? etc.
- Staging aspects – What do you think character X might do when they say their line? (getting up and walking over to the window, for example?) Where will character Y be looking as they speak? What will X be doing when Y says 'X! Stop sawing your friend in half!'? etc.
- What objects would we need to perform this section of the play?

It will be better if you work on an entire short text for the week during this section of the lesson, so the children follow the plot of a brief play.

WHOLE CLASS FOCUSED WORD WORK (15 MINS)

This can relate directly to the script work in a number of ways, e.g. compare the day's text to the same story written as a piece of prose with speech, etc. Words for looking (staring, blinking, frowning); words to describe how the character said something; etc.

GROUP WORK (20 MINS)

Guided group reading of play scripts – graded texts for each group, working with the same text for the week.

A different group works in the performance area each day during this time, if possible supported by yourself or a teaching assistant.

Teacher/TA works closely with each group once, preparing them for their work in the performance area the next day.

Groups can do focused written work, annotating their text with stage directions; exploring different verbs, adverbs and adverb phrases to describe how characters speak different lines.

PLENARY (10 MINS)

Groups who have been working in the performance area present their rehearsed, active, performed reading.

Teacher leads questioning re: emotions, reactions. 'How did X feel when Y said that? How could you tell?'

Focused observation by audience will concentrate on use of space, objects, gesture and tone of voice. The focus could change daily from one to the other of these.

Figure 2.1

The opening exercises in Chapter 6 on *Blodin the Beast* illustrate how this can be done by creating a script from a narrative text. This work is not approached as a technical exercise, as it would be if children were simply asked to convert a page of narrative dialogue into scripted form or vice-versa. Instead, the approach is one of physicalising the words on the page, playing with their dynamic qualities of pitch and rhythm as a way of embodying them into sound and movement. Each of the five units in this project begins, in fact, with a close reading of sections drawn from the text from which a dramatic script is created. The fact that this script need not be written down in any conventional format is neither here nor there. A dramatic script is first and foremost a guide to performance.

Blodin is the one example in this book of drama being created largely from the outside in rather than from the inside out. By this I mean that the children in effect create performance work from a written text as opposed to progressing through a drama as a lived experience. In this latter form of drama, often described as 'process drama' or 'drama in education', various genres of written material can intensify or deepen the drama work and can be experienced as children would experience them in the real social world.

So how does such reading material serve a real dramatic function and hence deepen children's involvement? Take a letter, for example. In some follow-up work to the story of *The Elves and the Shoemaker*, a group of five-year-old children, who have been playing the role of the elves, receive the following letter.[2]

Dear Elves

I am writing to you because I have heard that you help people with problems.

I am the owner of a circus. I have some baby monkeys that refuse to perform tricks for me.

I have tried hitting them with my stick and locking them in very small cages with nothing to eat or drink but they still won't do what I want.

Please can you make them do as they are told?

Yours truly,

George McNasty, circus owner

Figure 2.2

This letter does several things at once. It vividly sketches the image of a special kind of villain; it suggests a future line of action for the children as elves – the villain must be defeated and the monkeys rescued; and it has a highly ironic subtext – in asking for help in this way, Mr McNasty is actually guaranteeing that his plans will be thwarted. When the children meet a baby monkey (a glove puppet on the teacher's hand) they quickly realise that it has escaped from the circus. Although it can only nod or shake its head in answer to their questions, the children are able to find out enough information to give them an idea how to help set the other monkeys free. Remembering how drama thrives on secrets and lies, the children might consider writing a reply to Mr McNasty suggesting that they will be happy to help him but need to visit him first and see these monkeys and their cages for themselves. And, of course, where he keeps the keys to the cages . . .

In the above example, a letter is used as a pre-text to a drama. As a drama unfolds, a letter might be used to fill in details from a character's past; to suggest or reveal a secret; as a reply to an enquiry; as advice from a mysterious stranger; as an invitation to a secret meeting. The register in which it is written will depend upon whether it is formal or informal, written in the past or the present. As such, it can provide a writing frame for children to reply to should the requirements of the drama demand it.

Other genres of text for reading can be built into drama work. Some of the examples drawn from the units in this book include: a newspaper article, a sign in a garden, an entry in a private journal, a boat ticket in a foreign language, a visiting card, a map. In each case they mirror and hence provide models for the social uses of print. However, they are dramatically most effective when they are indeterminate and suggestive rather than precise and transparent. In other words, they capture children's imaginations primarily through what they suggest rather than through what they explain, when they contain a 'creative gap' for children to engage with, operating as clues rather than as reports. And it is this very gap that can help children learn to read texts critically as well as for their literal meanings.

A simple example of this is in the scheme on 'The Selfish Giant'. When the children have been playing in the garden they are surprised to see the sign 'Trespassers will be Prosecuted!' and even more surprised when they realise what it means (4:1c)! It leads them to ask a number of questions. Questions such as *Why has the giant decided that we can't play in his garden any more?* are stimulated by the lack of explanation given for the sign's appearance, the creative gap that this opens up. But the teacher can also lead children into asking a different type of question. *Why is the sign so big and the print so large, even by a giant's standards? Why has he written it in red?* In considering the intended effect of a specific text, how the giant is using and presenting language in a way that is meant to frighten them, children are critically engaging with text as they are exploring its use for socially manipulative purposes. Later in the drama (4:2b, c), they invent their own signs and present them in an appropriate physical and vocal manner. This is a fun activity that also furthers the aims of critical literacy as the children experiment and play symbolically with the potential power of print themselves.

Drama and writing

Drama will not teach children the basic skills of reading. It is not a good vehicle for teaching the rules of phonics. Its value in developing reading lies in the exciting contexts it can provide to simulate higher order skills of inferring meaning from text, of critically engaging with it and, where appropriate, of expressively articulating it. Similarly with writing; drama may provide contexts in which spelling and grammar can be seen to matter – as in the writing of a letter to someone powerful and influential – but it will not teach these skills. As I have argued, however, these skills are only a part of the English curriculum, a means to an end, not an end in themselves. If the children are to become effective writers they need to be able to do a lot more than manipulate the rules of grammar, spelling and punctuation. They need to be able to consider the effect and purpose of a piece of writing and choose not only appropriate vocabulary but also appropriate registers when they write.

The class teachers involved in the projects that form the substance of this book had the following observations to make on the positive effects they had seen drama have on their children's writing:

- It motivated more children to want to write;
- It provided more children with substantial ideas and experiences so that they had something to write about;
- Each child could draw individual responses from the drama. Consequently, despite the structure of a writing frame, individual pieces of writing were different and reflective of the child's rather than the teacher's thinking;
- Children generally wrote more and in a shorter period of time;
- Children's vocabulary and sentence structure was noticeably richer when their writing emerged from drama work;
- More children demonstrated a clearer sense of audience in their writing;
- More children demonstrated empathy for those whom they wrote about;
- Some children's writing could be seen to have benefited from the input that the visual qualities of drama had to offer.

Below are four pieces of children's writing drawn from each of the projects, together with a brief analysis of their qualities as writing and the contribution made by the drama work towards this.

In this unsupported piece of writing (3:5d), Clara shows a mastery of the full stop and the capital letter. She can spell the common words well and can use her knowledge of phonetics to write words she cannot yet spell in a way that is readable for her audience. These are what we might term the *surface* features of her

> One sad day I was with my mum. I hat to go away from the land. I went to Englind. I slept in a sdabl. Bfor I went to Englind I got on a boat and on a train. My mama got kinapdt. I srae some sorvuns. I was hunggri. The sorvuns gave me some food and dringck. They tod me some words. They tod me some jobs. They hidid me. A bad man came. The man was ugli. He had fin iys. The sorvuns sed to the bad man we havnt sin a litl boy. The man dropd a leter. I notisd the leter it sed collingwud house. I went to collingwud house. I srae my mum. The sorvnts came to collingwood house. They resgyoud my mum. Me and my mum wr happy.

Figure 2.3 Story writing – Clara, aged 5

writing, but drama tends to impact more readily on the *deeper* aspects, those concerned with the making of meaning. The drama has provided her with a story to tell and she tells it in a logical sequence and with great economy. All the details she includes, including the feelings of hunger and happiness, were visually represented in the drama scheme. Her sequencing is all the more impressive as it does not follow the plot of the drama, which was structured from the perspective of the servants and so began with the finding of the young boy, Lucien, in a stable. In the drama, the story of his escape from his own country only emerged later but Clara managed to synthesise these events into their actual chronology. The words *kidnapped* and *rescued* were used often within the drama. The ugly bad man had 'thin eyes', she writes, and the teacher told me how this reflected accurately my facial expression when I played him in 3:3d (although, personally, I dispute the term 'ugly'!). Clara also shows an ability to identify with the central character, to write from his perspective, even though her own role was that of a servant throughout the drama. A final important point is that Clara herself is German. She speaks German at home and has been living in England for just two years. This was noticeably the longest piece of work she had yet written.

> Dear Giant
> I am a garden expert. If you want information for your garden call an expert. Every sunny day you must water your flowers because they will dry in the sun. If you want to plant a flower you must get a plant and dig a hole and put the plant in. If you want service call a garden centre.
> From Mikey
> Garden expert

Figure 2.4 Letter writing – Mikey, aged 6

Mikey is a child judged to be in the middle ability range by his teacher. This unsupported piece of letter writing (4:4i) is short but impressive not only for the accuracy of its spelling and grammar but also for its register. In role as a garden expert, Mikey writes with some conviction and command of tone. The pieces of information he provides are apt and drawn from his understanding of the science work with which this drama was linked. The letter, written after a session in the imaginative play area, thus allows him to express scientific information appropriately within a specific social register.

Ferdinand gets justice by Prospro leting him marry Miranda. First of all Prospro did not let him marry her because he was the son of his enemy. And Ferdinands farther Alonzo wanted Prospro to not be Adrmal. Prospro found out that it was really his brothers idea his brother talked Alonzo into helping him. Antonio left Prospro on the planet because he wanted to be capton on the ship he left Prospros dater as well so Prospro had compony. In the end Prospro lets Ferdinand marry Miranda. I think it is just.

Figure 2.5 Reflective argument – Parpinder, aged 8

Like 80 per cent of the children in his class, Parpinder speaks a language other than English at home, in his case, Punjabi. He clearly has difficulties with *surface* elements such as spelling and punctuation but this should not blind us to the *deeper* merits of this as a piece of writing from an eight-year-old within a middle ability band. He was being asked to consider whether Ferdinand received Prospero's justice, forgiveness or revenge (5:5h). The writing is a clear example of how drama can help a child select and present concrete details – facts from the story – to illustrate their grasp of an abstract principle, in this case that of justice as distinct from revenge and forgiveness. In doing so, he is concise and accurate in his grasp of the plot, his choice of relevant detail and in his interpretation of the concept of justice. Although he does not spell it out, the implication is that, since Ferdinand's father, Alonzo, is less guilty than Prospero's brother for the wrongs Prospero has suffered, then it is only fair that he be lenient to Alonzo's son. Parpinder's sense of justice therefore appears to take a code of family honour seriously and the highly significant area of cultural values with relation to this project is explored in the final chapter.

The

blazing sun

settles in the

FIERY   **SKY**

SHARP FLAT MOUNTAINS STIFF AS CAN BE

infinite   sand dunes

            patterning

                        far   and   wide

sly scorpions s u   l e   towards their next VICTIM
            c t t

                                                hisssssing

            slender snakes

                    sliding   slithering

Figure 2.6 Landscape poetry – Ruth, aged 9

This remarkable piece of poetry was written on the computer in about 30 minutes. Ruth, a child assessed as above average by her teacher, drew upon the phrases that her group had developed from studying a section of written text in *Blodin the Beast* and the illustration that accompanied it (6:3e). The rhythm of these phrases had been used to create movement motifs to represent the desert. Ruth placed the images on the page to reflect where they had been performed in the space and chose the size of print to represent the dynamic of the vocal delivery of each. The colours she chose to reflect meaning – green for the snake, black for the scorpion, yellow for the sanddunes, brown for the mountains and red for the sun. As well as a poem, then, this piece of writing is a creative and effective performance script.

Beginning to use drama in your classroom

If you accept the argument that drama can and should play an integral part in your English teaching, there are immediate implications for your pedagogy, or the ways in which you teach. If you are less experienced or less confident, then the model lessons presented in Chapter 1 and in the later chapters may appear a little daunting. However, your pedagogy may be closer to drama than you realise. Before attempting such 'full-on' drama teaching you may, therefore, like to consider the following questions and, if necessary, follow some of the advice offered to build up your confidence. You will find teaching drama a lot easier than you think!

- *How often do you tell stories to your class?* Try developing your skills as a storyteller. Take a short folk tale or fable, read it a few times until you can improvise a telling of it then tell it rather than read it to your class. Try using your hands, objects, facial expression, tone of voice to emphasise meanings. Alternatively, do the same with a personal story, something that happened to you, embroidering the details and including dialogue.

- *How playful is your teaching?* Do you ever 'pretend' with your class that you don't know an answer, for example, or that you can't spell a word? Do you deliberately remember the events of a story wrongly so that the children have to put you straight? Such playful talk can be included in your everyday teaching and can prepare the way for the playful approaches of drama.

- *Do you ever take on simple roles with your class to give added purpose to a particular exercise?* A stranger who needs directions from a map during a geography topic? Or a difficult customer in a numeracy lesson on money calculations? Taking on such simple roles will help you realise that you don't need to be a great actor to make drama work for you. It is a straightforward development from this simple use of role to **hot-seating**, where you take on the role of a character for children to question.

- *How flexible is your classroom organisation?* Do you consciously use space and objects as part of your teaching? Present the class with a 'lost' bag or wallet containing clues to the owner's character to stimulate creative writing? Ask children to place a historical object along a time line? Ask them to organise themselves along a line depending upon how much they agree or disagree with a certain statement?

- *How good are you at giving non-verbal cues to children?* Can you convey feelings of disappointment, interest, excitement, satisfaction, pleasure, etc. through gesture and facial expression rather than words?

- *Do you have any playful methods for issuing-in certain routines that do not involve giving instructions?* For example, when you begin to recite a particular nursery rhyme, children might know that they are to join in, tidy their things and come and sit in front of you on the carpet in an orderly way.

- *Do you use circle time to engage children in open-ended and non-judgemental discussion of social and moral issues?*

- *How many of the building blocks of drama have you used as part of your teaching?* Some of these *conventions* are listed and described in Appendix 1. Try them out individually for the purposes suggested. Take care not to use the same few all of the time but make an effort to explore their possibilities and expand your expertise.

- *Do you feel that the schemes presented here or in other publications do not suit you or your particular circumstances?* Then adapt them to make them work for you!

Notes

1 E. Eisner (1969) cited in K. Robinson 'Evaluating TIE', in A. Jackson (ed.), *Learning through Theatre*, London, Routledge, 1993.
2 I am grateful to Miles Tandy for the inspiration to this drama.

Drama, English and citizenship

'Lucien and Marie – Refugees in Victorian Britain'

Context

Suitable for children between the ages of 5 and 8, this project was devised for a class of Year 1 children (aged 5 to 6) in a large suburban primary school with a substantial minority of pupils who spoke English as an Additional Language (EAL). The class was pursuing a history topic on the Victorians and had recently visited a large country house where they had spent some time in role as servants. Some knowledge of the Victorian way of life, particularly the life of servants, is, then, desirable before following the scheme, although the project itself provides opportunities to reinforce this knowledge. The work took place over five days in the classroom and took over approximately two hours of the morning timetable.

Outline of the drama

The children play the role of Victorian servants throughout the drama, with the teacher and/or teaching assistant introducing the roles of the different characters. Both the form and content of the drama draw heavily from nineteenth-century models. There is more than a touch of Dickens, Conan Doyle and Victorian melodrama here, although the story it contains is intended to have contemporary relevance. The drama begins as a normal day in Ruskin Manor with the household of Sir Roger and Lady Arnold. Sir Roger is a Member of Parliament and he and his wife are up in London until the end of the drama. The servants are being supervised by the housekeeper as they do their various jobs, when they discover a young boy asleep in one of the stables. He is tired, hungry and frightened and speaks only a few words in a language the servants do not understand. However, objects in his possession provide clues to his identity – a locket with a photograph of a woman; a letter; a ticket indicating that he has travelled from a French port. Through these, the appearance of a newspaper article and the mimed communication of the boy, the servants work out that he and his mother have had to flee their own country, coming to Britain to seek safety. However, his mother has been kidnapped and, escaping, the boy has wandered exhausted into their stable. The servants decide to help him, teaching him words of English and disguising him as one of the servants of the house. His name is Lucien and his mother's name is Marie. A strange man comes in search of Lucien and unwittingly leaves behind a clue as to where his mother is being held. The servants are able to help Lucien free her and learn that she is a journalist fleeing from political persecution in her own country for speaking out against an intolerant government. They intercede with Sir Roger on their behalf and the drama ends with their own speculations as to how they would like the story to conclude.

Note: The story is based upon historical fact, inasmuch as Britain prided itself as a safe haven for refugees in the nineteenth century, particularly during times of political unrest, such as the aftermath of the European revolutions of 1848. Chief among those who found refuge in Britain during this period were exiles from Italy, Poland and France.[1]

Learning intentions

1. To present a sympathetic portrait of people who may be forced to seek asylum in another country.

2. To raise non-EAL children's awareness of and esteem for other languages and language users.

3. *(if appropriate)* To raise EAL children's self-esteem through giving them real and symbolic high status in the drama.

4. In English
   - To describe incidents, ask and answer appropriate questions, listen with sustained concentration and consider courses of action;
   - To read for information;
   - To write instructions, to list questions; letter and story writing.

5. In Drama
   - To sustain work in role;
   - To respond appropriately to teacher in role;
   - To interpret and use gesture to convey meaning

6. In History and Geography
   - To reinforce knowledge of everyday life in Victorian times, with specific reference to household tasks, transport and dress;
   - To become acquainted with the use of globes, maps and plans.

Specific objectives

NLS	Y1/3: T5, 6, 13, 14
NC Speaking and listening Key Stage 1	1a, b, c, d, e, f; 2a, b, c, d, e; 3a, b, c, d, e; 4a, b, c; 6a, b; 8c, d; 9a, b; 10a, b, c; 11a, b, c
Speaking, listening, drama objectives	Y1: 1, 2, 3, 4, 5, 6, 7, 12
NC History Key Stage 1	1a; 2a; 3; 4b; 6b
NC Geography Key Stage 1	2c; 2e; 3e; 4a
NC PSHE and citizenship	1a, b; 2a; 4b, c, d, e

Roles and props/costume for the teacher

- Housekeeper (large bunch of keys; hat; candlestick (1f))
- Lucien (jacket, cap and/or scarf; small bag with clues to his identity)
- Marie (shawl)
- Mr Smith (cloak/top hat/cane)
- Porter (large key)
- Sir Roger (smart hat and/or gloves)

Note: You only need one or two items to signal your role, and it will help if they have a nineteenth-century appearance about them. These items of costume can become useful points of discussion by being compared to more modern items of dress in order to help develop children's sense of the past. For example, you might produce a smart top hat and a battered baseball cap and ask children to place them on the time line. They may well place the baseball cap as further back in time because it looks older, i.e. more worn.

UNIT 1

(a) Warm-up game: miming the servants' jobs

Introduce three jobs with distinct actions and levels, e.g. scrub the floor (children on knees); wipe the table (children stooping over); clean the window (children standing up straight). The children play to your commands. Then see if they can respond to silent instructions. Using no words, signal to the class to come towards you; to stop; to be quiet; to scrub the floors, etc. Can the class play this game again silently?

(b) Using the warm-up to introduce roles

Show children the prop that introduces you as the housekeeper and explain that whenever you wear, or hold it, you will be Mr(s) Hodgkiss. You are interviewing for servants who can do their work efficiently and energetically for Sir Roger and Lady Atkins. Be firm but kind in your role. Repeat the first game, this time in role, making encouraging comments. In the mornings, all these jobs need to be done in absolute silence so as not to awaken the master and his wife. Still in role, repeat the silent game. At the end, praise the servants and say that they will all get jobs.

(c) Studying a plan of the house

Show children a photograph and a simple plan of the house in which they will be working as servants.[2] Talk about what rooms/areas they can see; read the names; discuss whether various rooms/areas are up or downstairs, inside or outside. Then revise what they know about the jobs that need doing in different parts of the house.

(d) Group work : working in different parts of the house

Put children into groups and allocate each to a different area – kitchen; laundry room; dining room; bedrooms; stables and outbuildings. Exactly how you organise this will depend upon how much prior work the children will have done on Victorians. They will very likely need adult intervention to help them play at the various tasks. You may set each group on an initial task before visiting each in turn as the housekeeper to encourage or help them and to allocate individual tasks within the groups. The tasks ought to be as authentic as is reasonable to reinfoce the difference between then and now.

Laundry: boiling the copper; using the 'dolly' and 'posser'; grating the soap; fetching water from the well; scrubbing collars; wringing clothes through the mangle; hanging laundry in the drying room.

Kitchen: gathering fuel for the oven and lighting it; boiling a kettle on the fire to make tea; chopping meat and vegetables; washing the pots.

Dining room: lighting the fire; sweeping the floors; replacing the table linen; polishing and laying out the silver; laying the table.

Bedrooms: lighting the fires; changing the bed linen; bringing in the water jugs; emptying the chamber pots!

Stables and outbuildings: brushing down and feeding the horses; changing the hay; sweeping the courtyard; polishing saddles and stirrups.

(e) Group performance: showing how well the servants work

As the housekeeper, invite the other servants to see in turn how well each group is working. Ask about individual tasks so that each group can explain a little about what jobs they are doing. Praise each group for their very good work before moving on.

(f) Narration into action: who is the young boy?

Sit the children in a circle and narrate how Mr(s) Hodgkiss came to the servants one night holding a candle. She had heard a noise coming from the stables and wanted them to go and investigate. Choose two volunteers, bring them into the circle and give one of them the candle. Narrate how they went quietly down into the stable, adding atmospheric touches – the doors creaking open, etc. – and quietly approached a figure lying asleep on the hay. Become that figure as you narrate. *It was a young boy wearing a scarf and a cap, lying down on the hay. In front of him was a small bag . . . He was fast asleep (pause).* Take off the scarf and cap, ask a child to wear them and to lie perfectly still next to the bag. In a hushed voice, ask what we can tell about this boy from looking at him. Ask questions such as *Why do you think he is wearing a scarf? Why do you think he is sleeping in a stable?* Then ask if they think his bag might have some clues as to who he is. *Would it be all right for us to look inside? We won't steal it! Does anyone want to get it for me without waking the boy up . . .?* Once you have the bag, look inside, show a puzzled expression and stop the drama!

(g) Discussion: how things have changed!

Can the children help you list five examples or more, at least one example from each group, of how jobs are done differently in our homes today?

(h) Writing about the servants' jobs

Children can be asked to write simple sentences to describe their jobs, or these can be framed to develop specific literacy objectives. Prepositions can be particularly challenging for EAL children, so, in the class where this project was developed, differentiated cloze procedure tasks concentrated on these, despite the fact that they are not specified in the National Literacy Strategy for children of this age. More able children were presented with a detailed narrative of a servant's day with all the prepositions removed and presented at the top of the page. Children in the middle ability range were given a set of six commands to complete.

e.g.

Get the chamber pot from . . . the bed

on
over
under

Children in the lower ability groups had cards on which different prepositions were written. They used each to make up different sentences about the jobs, which the teaching assistant scribed for them.

UNIT 2

(a) Examining the clues to the boy's identity

The bag should contain three items: a locket with the picture of a well-dressed Victorian woman inside; a boat ticket for two from Calais to Dover (see Figure 3.1); and the fragments of a simple handwritten letter (Figure 3.2). A simple sketch of a ship on the ticket will indicate that it is a boat ticket.

Billet pour deux personnes
Calais (France) à Douvres
(Angleterre)

Figure 3.1

Dear Marie
I wish you a safe journey to England. Do take care as not everyone in this country will welcome you.
    I am looking forward to seeing your son, Lucien, for the first time. Is he seven yet?
Your good friend
Kate

Figure 3.2

Discuss with the children what these items might be telling us about the boy and his circumstances. It will help if you have already prepared larger versions of the ticket and letter to read through. Speculate as to the language it is written in. You will be able to guide the children into a realisation that this is a ticket and can consult a globe or any large map to guide them into finding France. By asking children about their own knowledge of other countries, particularly the experiences of any EAL children in your class, you can locate their own countries of origin and discuss how they travelled to Britain, how long it took, etc., comparing it to Lucien's journey.

Note: this discussion is speculative and is intended to raise questions. What is his language? Does anyone here recognize it? Who is the woman? Where might she be now? etc.

(b) Warm-up: jobs in the stable

Not wishing to disturb the boy, the servants work quietly around him. Recollect what the stable jobs were, then at your silent commands, play a similar game to (1b).

(c) Questioning Lucien

Ask the children how as servants they can show they are friendly, so as not to frighten the boy. Remember, he may not understand English. Narrate how he wakes up and, in role as Lucien, look slightly frightened, warming to the servants' friendliness. Then tell them your name and mime that you are hungry and want food and drink, nodding and saying 'Oui!' when children guess correctly. When you start to eat, smile, offer food and drink to the servants and then come out of role. Now that he has eaten, do you think we can ask our questions? Encourage children to realise that, as he can't speak English, they will need to find other ways of communicating. Will the items in the bag help? Work out together some ways we can use body language – pointing at the picture and looking puzzled, etc. When they are ready, go back into role as Lucien, watch the children's questions carefully then mime your story in response: your boat journey; catching a train with your mother; a big man with a stick arriving and dragging your mother from a train into a horse drawn carriage; how your mother threw her bag to you as you escaped. Do this like a game of charades, moving on to the next part only when they have more or less grasped the story so far. It will be a lot of fun and it does not matter yet if the children misunderstand some of the story.

It will help if you use some French words to accompany your actions. Basic

French phrases such as *du pain/de l'eau, s'il vous plaît; un homme à chapeau; le sac de ma mère,* etc. will suffice.

(d) Working in pairs: Lucien pretends to be a servant

Out of role, question children about what they think they have learned from Lucien. Ask them if we might be able to hide him. Could we teach him the servants' jobs so well that Mr(s) Hodgkiss will think he is one? Put the class in pairs so that each is with a servant from a different area of the house than their own. Each is to play Lucien in turn. First one teaches the other how to do their job, then vice versa. Can they do each job exactly together so that we can't tell which is Lucien? Tour as Mr(s) Hodgkiss and be suitably deceived.

(e) What English phrases could we teach Lucien?

Ask the children to imagine that Lucien was starting at their school. What do they think would be the ten most important phrases for him to learn? After discussing a few initial examples as a whole class, children might work on making a list in their literacy groups.

(f) What we learned from the objects

Make differentiated worksheets showing pictures of the ticket, the photo and the letter. Alongside each, children are to write what they now know about them.

UNIT 3

(a) Game: Keeper of the Newspaper!

Narrate how the servants saw Mr(s) Hodgkiss with a newspaper with the headline 'Woman and Boy Dragged from Train'. Who could they be? Might we learn something if we read the newspaper? Play a version of **Keeper of the Keys** to get the newspaper from her.

(b) Reading a newspaper article

Show the children the full version of the article, written up on a flip chart or projected large (see Figure 3.3). Read this together and discuss what it is telling us. The text can be adapted to suit the reading abilities of your class.

WOMAN AND BOY DRAGGED FROM TRAIN

A woman and a small boy have gone missing from a train travelling from Dover to London.

The train had stopped at a station when suddenly a man dragged them from it.

Witnesses saw them being thrown into a carriage pulled by two horses and driven away.

The man was tall and dressed in a long black cape and a tall hat. He was carrying a cane.

Passengers on the train say that the woman spoke good English but that she and her son spoke Fench together.

The woman was dressed in *(here include details that fit the photo in the locket).* The boy was wearing *(here include details of the costume you have been using as Lucien).*

None of the witnesses understands why they have been kidnapped.

Figure 3.3

Figure 3.4 Pupils in role as Lucien and his mother on the train

c) Group mime: hiding Lucien

Ask the class if we could hide Lucien should the man come looking for him here. Model how you can mime hiding in a cupboard. This will help stop children running under tables or behind curtains. In their servant groups, children are to think of a good place where he could hide in their area and, at the call 'Hide!' one of them is to pretend to be Lucien as the others help him hide. From their actions we should be able to tell where this is. Go around and help each group before they show the rest of the class. Discuss how we could tell where Lucien was hiding in each case.

Figure 3.5 Child as Mr Smith

(d) Teacher in role

Children sit in a circle as you narrate that there came a knock on the door. Lucien was hiding, as a tall man in a black cape and hat and holding a cane was shown in. Ask the children who they think he is. If he asks you any questions, do you think you can avoid telling him that Lucien is hiding here? Then put on the costume and give the children an insincere smile. Introduce yourself as Mr Smith. You are looking for a missing boy. You are a friend of his mother's and she is very worried about him. Can they help you? Are they sure they haven't seen him? You have heard that he was last seen near here, etc. Push the children with your questioning as though you are not sure whether you believe them or not. When you feel it is right to stop, narrate, So Mr Smith turned to leave but as he did so, he mistakenly dropped a card on to the floor . . .

(e) Game

A short, lively game may be useful here to release energy before focusing the children on the clue that has been left.

(f) What does the card tell us?

Sit children in the circle and quietly replace the card where it dropped on the floor. Start questioning the children about Mr Smith and pretend to notice the card only when they draw your attention to it. It is a calling card with an address, Collingwood House. Who do we think Mr Smith is? Might Lucien's mother be held prisoner there? Should we look at a map and see if we can find it?

(g) Studying a map

Have a simple map using picture symbols prepared for display. It can show Ruskin Manor in one corner and Collingwood House in the other. Between them there should be a series of simple geographical features – a hedge or fence round the gardens; a bridge over a river; a tunnel under a railway track; a wood; etc. Have children study the route and describe how to get From Ruskin Manor to Collingwood House using prepositions throughout. 'Go out of the door and down the steps. Walk across the garden, crawl under the hedge. Cross over the bridge and walk down into the tunnel', etc.

(h) Prepositions and writing instructions

Discuss when might be the best time to go and secretly investigate Collingwood House (night time, of course!). Show proudly how you have already written down the instructions to get there. Start to read through them. It becomes obvious that they are seriously wrong, for you have written things like: 'Go down the door and under the steps', etc. Fortunately you have prepared sheets for the children to complete their own sets of instructions, which they do as a cloze procedure exercise.

(i) Letter from Lucien

Say how good the servants have been in teaching Lucien and that his English is much improved. In fact he was very interested in their work and studied the map and read their instructions very carefully. He's written you something, you think he has had a go at what they have been doing, shall we read it? Open it and look shocked. Ask a child to read it. It says. 'Thank you my friends and goodbye. I have gone to Collingwood House to find my mother.' Oh no! What do you think the servants will want to do now?

UNIT 4

(a) Warm-up: going to Collingwood House

Explain that if we are to go to Collingwood House together we don't want to be seen. How good are the children at moving silently through space? Narrate the journey and move through the space with them. Use expressive vocabulary. Talk very quietly and ask for their help at times. *First, we creep through the door and tip-toe down the steps. Where do we go now, can anyone remember?* etc. Once at the house, gather the children and sit them down.

(b) Talk in role: trying to get past the porter

Narrate how a stern-looking man approached the gates and saw the servants. He held a big key in his hand — the key to all the rooms, including the one where Lucien's mother would be. What shall we say to this man to persuade him to let us in? Once the children have some reasonable ideas, become the porter, listen to them, ask them questions in return. But you are bigoted. Mr Smith is a good man, an Englishman. Yes, you have seen him with a woman. You don't like her, she is obviously not from these parts and doesn't belong here. She's one of these foreign troublemakers and you hope Mr Smith is going to put her on a boat and send her straight back home. Yes, you have seen a pest of a boy here, too. You chased him. You think he was stupid because he couldn't speak English properly. Stop things when appropriate by saying. *The porter left them outside the gate and went back to his seat at the door of the house. The servants watched as he sat down and fell asleep.*

(c) Game: Keeper of the Keys

Ask the children if anyone spotted a way into the gardens other than through the gate. Some children are bound to have ideas. Choose one of them, quietly make your way into the garden and ask children to sit in a circle. Play **Keeper of the Keys** to get the key from the porter.

(d) Game: movement and stillness

Once we get into the house we need to explore it but we don't want Mr Smith to see us, do we? Children are to search quietly through the space, but each time you call 'Mr Smith!' they are to freeze and remain still. Then, outside one of the doors, they see someone they know very well . . .

(e) Physicalising Lucien's mother

Call the children together and, in role as Lucien, explain to them quietly and in hesitant English how you climbed in through an open window, have searched the corrridors and have found a room with a locked door. You are sure your mother is being kept there. If only you had a key. But of course, the servants have it! Send a child quietly to open the door and ask for another to volunteer to be Lucien's mother. Ask the class to show what they think she will do when she sees Lucien at the door. Tell the volunteer that they can choose from any ideas offered if they are helpful. Narrate how Lucien put the key in the lock and slowly turned it and let's see how his mother reacted when she saw him. You can run this a few times with different children each time.

(f) Game: being chased by Mr Smith

Sit the children in a circle and narrate how, at that minute when everyone was so happy, a big shout was heard. It was Mr Smith! The servants ran off with Lucien's mother but he began to chase Lucien. Ask for a volunteer. Give her Lucien's hat to wear and whisper to her not to worry, you won't catch her. Then say to the class, *Shall we see if Mr Smith can catch Lucien?* and begin to chase the child around the circle clumsily, swinging a rolled-up piece of paper as your cane, falling over, perhaps, getting close but never touching her. Ask other children if they would like to take on either role. Each time, whisper to the child who plays Mr Smith that the trick is not to catch or hit Lucien. Run this three or four times.

(g) Listing questions and hot-seating Marie

What things can Marie tell us that we still don't know? List some questions with the children. For example, why did they have to leave their country? Who is Mr Smith? Why did he kidnap her? Then let the children hot-seat you in role. Tell them that there has been fighting in your country over who should be in charge. You are a journalist, you write in newspapers. You disagree with the way your country's new leader wants to put people who don't like him into prison. You wrote about this and now he wants to put you in prison, too. Mr Smith called you a troublemaker. He has told people working for the government of your country where you are and he was waiting for someone to come and take you back. Now you are very afraid what will happen to you and you don't know if you will be allowed to stay in this country.

(h) Writing a letter to Sir Roger

Do the servants think Lucien and Marie should stay in this country? Could they write a letter to Sir Roger, asking if he can help? After all, he is a Member of Parliament. Explain what that means. Write the letter together. It need not tell him everything but should be persuasive enough for him to want to come and talk to the servants. Children can help you decide how best to do this.

(i) Circle time – what do we think of the porter?

Ask children to recall some of the things that the porter said. Do we agree with them? For example, is Lucien stupid? In what ways has he shown that he is clever? Has Marie come here to cause trouble? etc.

UNIT 5

(a) Warm-up: Mr Smith tag!

Using the hat, whichever child wears it is Mr Smith. Any child he tags must stay still until released by another child. Switch the hat to another child at any point.

(b) Teacher in role: meeting Sir Roger

Gather the children together and explain that Sir Roger has arrived back and wishes to talk to the servants. Thank them for their letter then question them so that you get the full story of Lucien and Marie. Make them work hard to convince you of its truth, telling them that your country is proud to welcome people who are being persecuted in their own countries. That they can stay so long as they do not break the laws of this country. That Mr Smith has no right to do what he is doing. That *he* is the troublemaker as he is the one breaking the law in this case. Tell the children/servants that you would like to make a speech in Parliament about how we should and should not treat people like Lucien and Marie who come to our country seeking our help. Will they help you note down some ideas? Do this together on the flipchart.

(c) Freeze frame: how do we want the story to end?

Talk to the children about how they think the story ought to end for Lucien and Marie and for Mr Smith. Discuss different possibilities for suitable endings, then put them into pairs and ask them to create photographs that illustrate them. Show and discuss.

(d) Write and illustrate the story

Children should now be able to write and illustrate their own versions of the story. (See Chapter 2, Figure 2.3) More able children should need minimal support for this activity.

Figure 3.6

(e) A final letter from Lucien

Basing your writing on the children's preferred ideas in (5c), produce a letter from Lucien to the servants (written large) which tells them what has happened to himself, his mother and Mr Smith. Read through and discuss it with the children.

(f) Display: reflecting upon the story

Make a display showing how the servants made Lucien and Marie welcome in their country. Alongside it make another display about the people whom we should make welcome to our school and what we can do to make them feel welcome.

A trivial local drama?

While I was in the process of writing this book, the local television station ran an item on the regional nightly news programme. It covered a disagreement over a pantomime due to be performed in a village not far from the school where this project was taught. The long tradition of performing it in the local church hall was being disrupted as the church committee had disapproved of this year's script. Entitled *Snow White and the Seven Asylum Seekers*, the prospective panto featured characters with names such as 'Back Ali' and 'Bowling Ali' and depicted them as living in squalor and sponging off the state. The report treated the issue in a light-hearted manner, as a trivial local dispute, adopting the form of the pantomime itself to mirror the disagreement in the village. For example, after the voice-overs 'Oh no it shouldn't!' and 'Oh yes it should!' various locals expressed their opinions as to whether the panto either should or should not go ahead. Those who supported it seemed to outnumber those who didn't, regarding it as a 'harmless bit of fun' and the arguments that it might be offensive as 'political correctness gone mad'. One woman also pointed out how the profits from the panto were always given to charity and that it was a great shame that those in need would suffer as a result of any decision to cancel it.[3]

The anecdote is pertinent to this chapter for a number of reasons beyond the evident thematic connection. It shows how very young children can be exposed to stories and representations that vilify minority social groups currently classed as 'undeserving' in the popular imagination. It illustrates how many issues dealing with social and moral values are deeply contentious and have an inescapable political dimension to them that teachers cannot always avoid. It therefore raises the question as to whether as teachers we believe that schools should counter such stories and, if so, how. The patronising tone of the media was, for me, troubling, reinforcing an argument in favour of the teaching of critical literacy, as expressed in the last chapter. Finally, the very fact that it was a piece of theatre causing the upset, in a form that is popular and aimed at young children, is particularly telling. Not only does it remind us of how children can be exposed to and also be the direct targets of messages that embrace populist and controversial values, it is indicative of the power of drama to bring value-related issues, wittingly or unwittingly, into the public domain. These issues lie at the heart of this essay, which will examine the role of drama within values education, specifically within the context of citizenship, where social and moral values inevitably take on a political dimension.

Citizenship and social and moral education

Citizenship is a recent arrival as an educational concept and follows its re-emergence in the early 1990s as an issue of interest to both political philosophers and politicians.[4] Now a statutory part of the curriculum in the UK the guidance divides it into three related areas, those of social and moral responsibility, community involvement and political literacy all linked officially under the heading *Personal, Social and Health Education and Citizenship*.[5] The first two of the three related areas have a long and active tradition in primary schools whereas the third area, that of political literacy, is documented so as largely to be the concern of secondary education. However, as the above anecdote shows, in the public domain, it can be extremely difficult to separate the moral from the political, even in the lives of young children.

Both PSHE and citizenship are deeply concerned with values, with concepts of the good and of being good. In PSHE children learn ethical values that the school and the community wish them to share in common – the importance of honesty;

why we shouldn't steal or tell lies, etc. The truth is, of course, that as children grow, they will find that many of these values, often learned as simple rules, will at times clash. Should I tell the teacher that it was my friend who broke the window? Such might be an example of an early moral dilemma for a child, where they are torn between two ethical principles, loyalty and honesty. A moral education, therefore, as well as teaching children agreed forms of ethical codes, is also intended to help them think their way through difficult moral dilemmas, to cope with value complexity. This aspect of moral education deals with shared values and embraces what we might call the intimate zone of the individual's own conscience. An education for citizenship is also intended to help children deal with complex issues of conflicting values but is explicitly about values in the public domain. At its heart is a democratic ideal, that of teaching children to value a system in which a plurality of values will be allowed to gain expression and can be debated and acted upon rationally in a public arena. Within this concept of citizenship, the ideas of Hannah Arendt can provide us with a theoretical framework in which drama education might play a significant role.

Hannah Arendt's theory of citizenship

The following summary of Arendt's ideas is taken from the essay by Passerin d'Entreves referred to above.[6] They are very condensed but, I hope, sufficient and sufficiently clear to support the analysis that ensues.

1. Citizenship is about values that shape action in the public sphere. This public sphere requires structures that allow individuals to be seen and heard, to come together for collective discourse while maintaining their own identities as moral agents. In other words, it is a place where we must look and be looked at, speak and listen to others speak, seek common cause while acknowledging our individual differences.

2. The public sphere is therefore a 'space of appearance'. But it is also a 'world we hold in common'. This world is a cultural one, constructed by humans. We find it in the institutions that allow democracy to flourish and also in those human artefacts that enable what we hold in common to be preserved across generations. Hence works of art, the stories that we tell ourselves about ourselves, both fictional and historical, help sustain this world.

3. The world we hold in common is not essentially a world of common values, it is more a shared world of political institutions and common practices. Arendt's analogy is that of a dining table. The table provides each of the diners with an individual space that also places them in relationship with one another. It is this shared space rather than some inner personal quality that unites them in a common purpose.

4. Self-interest and the common good will often clash. If I am called upon to serve on a jury, then it may well be very inconvenient to my personal and business interests. However, in agreeing to take up this role of civic responsibility, I can learn to appreciate my own role in the common good and transcend my own immediate self-interest.

5. Civic and political action is necessarily collective and involves answering not only the question 'What shall we do?' but also the question 'Who do we mean by "we"?' Within a democracy, it allows people from different backgrounds and with different histories and values to find common cause and act collectively.

6. Political thought is representative. In Arendt's words: 'I form an opinion by considering a given issue from different viewpoints, by making present to my mind the stand-points of those who are absent' (quoted in Passerin d'Entreves, 1992: 163). The better I am able to feel and think as though I were in the place of others, the better will be my thinking and the more valid my opinion.

7. People need to be schooled in citizenship, in the skills and values that enable them to sustain effective participation and to develop their moral imaginations. In Benhabib's words:

> The cultivation of one's moral imagination flourishes in such a culture in which the self-centred perspective of the individual is constantly challenged by the multiplicity and diversity of perspectives that constitute public life. (Passerin d'Entreves 1992: 164)

Such a perspective on the nature of citizenship suits well the cultural pluralism that increasingly characterises the contemporary globalised world. For at the heart of Arendt's idea is the principle of promoting institutions that can enable people to forge agreements and sustain common cause while retaining individual differences. So whatever my religion, ethnicity or class, what matters is that I come to understand and value the principles that can enable me to discourse and act with others in the public domain. Using these points to create a theoretical framework, we can now examine their relevance to the practices and values of drama education in general and see how they are illustrated in this drama in particular.

Drama and citizenship education

Drama and the public sphere: being seen and heard

Much of a child's life in primary school, in accordance with the old proverb, is about being seen but *not* heard – or at least, only being heard within strictly controlled structures. As we have seen, by its very nature, drama has the potential to loosen these controls and provide children with opportunities to be seen *and* heard and this potential is manifest at a number of levels.

- Its formal structures provide a space for groups to perform and watch others perform and can thus help children develop the confidence and skills needed to watch and listen to one another, as well as watch and listen to the teacher.

- Drama can provide a voice to those who are not usually heard. This is true both at the level of classroom discourse, where formal structures and the mask of a different identity can encourage quiet children to speak; and at the fictional level, as in this drama, where marginalised voices can be forced to the centre of attention.

- The use of role can help teachers obscure their own value position, or play devil's advocate. By deliberately taking on a role that is needy (2c) or provocative (4b), it can encourage children to express opinions, to debate and argue and to pit their wits against an opposing position.

Although this drama was developed for very young children, it presents formal opportunities for them to watch and be watched by their peers (1e; 2d; 3c; 4e; 4f; 5c). Importantly, the structure of these activities provides a double layer of protection for them, to foster self-confidence: in addition to the mask of role, they are protected from criticism. At no point need the teacher or the class give any negative verbal response to their public presentations. And to encourage children to look outward, to help harness their attention away from themselves, each activity has a game-like quality, or challenge for the spectator: What jobs are the servants doing? (1e); Which child is Lucien? (2d); Will Mr Smith catch Lucien? (4f).

With younger children, the opportunities for them to speak and listen in drama will generally take place in more improvised, less rehearsed scenarios, and the traditional drama shape, of everyone sitting in a circle, symbolically contracts them into an egalitarian, sharing ideal. This is particularly important in activities (such as 2c; 3d; 5b) where, although the teacher in different roles is necessarily focusing and motivating the discussion, the children's active watching, listening and responding is crucial for the activity to become both dramatic and educational. So, for example, unless Sir Roger forces the children/servants to work hard to convince him, neither the drama nor the learning will succeed. In other words, these particular skills, needed for the children to do successful drama, can contribute equally to their becoming successful citizens.

The voice that children are being asked to listen to in this drama is, of course, that of someone who needs their help. The fact that most young children will respond positively towards Lucien is due to very human reasons: their innate human potential to feel for others[7] and the fact that, when they meet him, he is relatively helpless, providing them with a rare, albeit fictional, opportunity to be powerful and enabling. All children are being encouraged to find common cause with Lucien and his mother and to appreciate the injustice they have suffered. But in this particular classroom there was a further aim, to give voice to the EAL children, not by simplifying their own identities and conflating them with Lucien's but by creating a context in which their own experiences and personal stories became particularly relevant and needed to be heard (2a; 2e; 5f).

Drama and the world we hold in common

Since its origins in ancient Greece, western drama has been a space of appearance, where the values that a culture perpetrates can be held up to public scrutiny. Like a political arena, it can be constructed in order to bring issues of value conflict to the fore. For example, we proclaim our society as one that upholds the rule of law, but how far is this true? When G. F. Newman's series *Law and Order* appeared on British TV channels in the late 1970s, offering a perspective on the law enforcement process that suggested elements of corruption at every level, public reaction was vociferous and the issue became the focus of national attention. Many powerful dramas offer this kind of challenge to social values, asking the question, are we as good as we think we are?

In a very simple way, this drama attempts something similar, presenting children with a story that offers a particular perspective on a current political story, different from its dominant representation in many parts of the media. It is also self-evidently an attempt to encourage certain values, in particular, those of tolerance, compassion and solidarity. Stories of all kinds, whether in newspapers, books or comics, whether on TV or cinema screens, whether fact or fiction, inescapably embody cultural and moral values. Stories are a key means not only of endorsing or challenging aspects of the world we have in common but also of educating us into it. But this world is never a stable world; these values are never fixed and unassailable. Rather they are constantly shifting and evolving, and democratic societies recognize this kind of struggle as inherently necessary in order to sustain a changing society that seeks to provide the ideals of justice and freedom for all. In a very small way, this drama is intended to engage children in a simple struggle that mirrors these ideals.

The Victorian era has long been seen as a good historical period for providing drama pretexts for children between the ages of 7 and 11. Stories of child labour, in particular, have been used to create excellent schemes of work that also introduce children to the political frameworks that enabled its injustices to be challenged.[8] This drama, planned for a younger class with a specific minority social group, chose a different way to dialogue with the past, setting it at a time when the British government had a more liberal attitude to those seeking political asylum than it displays today. By developing a melodramatic story, resonant of Victorian fiction but a form still widely popular, it nonetheless has its roots in historical fact.

A shared world, not an intimate world

Arendt maintains that in a democracy we can all hold different values provided that we value the political structures that permit us to express and debate them. This does necessitate that certain values *must* be shared, in particular, the values of freedom and social justice that lie at the root of democracy. Examining the complexity of these values is far beyond my capabilities or my present focus, but this inescapable fact does resonate with some tensions at the heart of drama education practice. Contracting has long been used to set the boundaries of what is acceptable in drama lessons, and by contracting-in certain helpful types of behaviour, we contract out others. Harmful, hurtful, insulting and personalised expressions are unacceptable in the drama classroom, as in any classroom. But what about within the drama itself? How far in improvised drama are we prepared to allow the voices of racism, fascism, sexism, prejudice and intolerance find expression within our classrooms within fictional frameworks? And how open will our agenda be if we *do* decide to give them a voice?

This particular drama does what many educational dramas do: it takes a safe line, setting up a voice of intolerance with clear connotations that it should not be listened to. In (4b) the porter expresses his prejudices in mild but clear language and in (4i) the children are encouraged to discuss why he is wrong. This is a clear example of value indoctrination, of the teacher identifying the primacy of particular virtues – or particular vices, in this case those of bigotry and prejudice – and deploying a strategy to encourage a specific stance towards them. The structure does not allow for the porter's prejudice to be heeded, as the children/servants are very clearly on the side of Lucien by now. So, in an attempt to further democratic values, the teacher here is in a sense asked to be undemocratic. This paradox can cause problems with older children as they will often see through and challenge such manipulative pedagogy.[9] In the case of younger children, however, I tend to agree with Bettelheim in the belief that they benefit from stories where the moral world of good and bad is clearly demarcated.[10]

There is a further layer of tension here. The drama space is separate from but intrinsically related to the social world that surrounds it. It enables not only reflective distance but also identity distance from my everyday self. When children speak and act in drama, they are not necessarily speaking and acting their own intimate thoughts. At the bottom of it all, drama remains playful. So when we judge what children actually say and do in this space we must be careful not to read too much into what values they will take away from it. Just as the child who spends ten minutes being monstrous can return and sit quietly at her desk, so can the child who has just spent half an hour being nice to Lucien run into a playground and kick someone. I actually believe that positive social behaviour patterns can be learned from drama work but, within the parameters of citizenship education, we can permit ourselves to concentrate upon the *public display* of values that occur within the space of appearance that is the drama lesson itself. Once again, this display can be evidenced at two levels, the actual and the fictional. In the actual framework, we can observe whether children are listening, watching, sharing, engaging; and at the fictional level we can introduce situations where they experience the formality of such frameworks within social and political situations beyond the classroom – the public meeting, the courtroom, the council chamber. Here the meeting with Sir Roger (5b) is significant as it introduces the children to a figure of authority beyond that of the teacher or headteacher, providing them with a fictional context and purpose for a formal exchange with him.

Collective action and the common good

As a communal form of art making, drama can provide opportunities for children to learn the importance of collective endeavour, the times when it is necessary to sacrifice their immediate self-interest for the good of a shared enterprise. This can be true at the level of a major production, where rehearsal times place demands upon children when they may well have other immediate preferences; and in class group work, where individuals need to learn to compromise in group decision-making. Of course, there are important pedagogical issues here, to ensure that the production, for example, is owned by the children and not just the teacher; and that the most forceful children are not always the ones who get their own way. But the reality is that such collective endeavour will always involve struggle, to find a common voice as well as a common cause. The important thing is to find value in the struggle, not simply to avoid it.

As dramatic action often mirrors action in the social world, a need to find a common cause and act together can be incorporated into the fiction itself. This is a common strategy in primary drama, enabled by whole class structures such as formal meetings. The younger the children, the more they will tend to act in one voice and the more they will need the teacher to test this voice, to engage it in struggle. Different interests and values will always be competing within a political arena and it is too much to expect young children to understand and represent them without guidance. This drama contains numerous examples of this kind of testing, the most significant of which, once again, is (5b) where the children, albeit in fiction, engage with a figure of political authority. As Sir Roger, the teacher will need to be convinced about the truth of the servants' story. He may well wonder if Marie can make money and look after herself in this country, if Lucien ought to be sent away to boarding school. He might speculate that perhaps they are ready to return to France after their unhappy experiences so far. He can wonder all of these things not because it is *right* that he should but because it is only in doing so that the children/servants will learn the struggle of collective endeavour in responding to him.

As servants, the social status of the children's role in this drama is unified and relatively low. Yet they are still encouraged to find a 'we' beyond the one social group, incorporating eventually their employer as well as Lucien and his mother. In other dramas and particularly with older children there is no reason why they cannot take on more socially powerful roles. With the mantle of the expert they can become doctors, scholars, researchers, detectives, people with knowledge, influence and power who can still encounter struggle within the public arena while searching for a just course of action.

Developing empathy through representation

If I am to 'make present in my mind the standpoints of others who are absent', the moral imagination that I am called upon to develop is one where empathy is paramount. Neelands has argued that when acting in drama 'the boundaries between self and other meet and merge'.

> the core of our humanity, the essence of compassion, the beginnings of morality are to be found in our capacity to merge 'self' with 'other'. (2002: 8)[11]

No other curriculum subject places such a high priority upon developing empathy, upon appreciating the common humanity we share with one another. As an actor who plays a character, I must find what I share with them to turn that character into flesh and blood, no matter how distant I feel they are from my own personal identity. But I need not be a 'good' actor. Arendt is talking of being able to represent someone's opinions in one's mind, knowing what they might think or say. Children here see Lucien and his mother then report to Sir Roger. In role as Marie they will have seen you happy to be reunited with your son, sad as you remember having to leave your country. As Lucien they have seen you frightened and lonely, happy to share their friendship, happier still to find your mother. Sir Roger might ask them whether they think Marie would mind if Lucien was sent off to a boarding school away from her; or how Lucien might feel if they allowed his mother to stay but sent him back to France. However the children/servants respond, he asks why they think that. Such simple devices can provide the platform for empathetic thought as well as help children begin to understand the multiplicity of perspectives that make up the public world.

Notes

1 See B. Porter, *The Refugee Question in Mid-Victorian Politics*, Cambridge, Cambridge University Press, 1979.

2 Photographs of Victorian mansions and Victorian women (2a) can readily be found on the internet via a Google image search. The plan is best drawn by yourself and need only show two floors.

3 The continuing story of this dispute also made the national press, with reports in the *Guardian* on 4 and 27 November and 4 December 2003.

4 See M. Passerin d'Entreves, 'Hannah Arendt and the Idea of Citizenship', in C. Mouffe (ed.), *Dimensions of Radical Democracy*, London, Routledge, 1992, p. 145.

5 See www.dfes.gov.uk/citizenship

6 I am very grateful to Jonothan Neelands for introducing me to this essay. His own writings on the significance of Hannah Arendt's contribution to a theory of citizenship and drama education are currently in preparation.

7 This is what Aristotle referred to as children's *orectic* potential. See J. Winston, *Drama, Narrative and Moral Education*, London, Falmer, 1998: p. 66.

8 See, for example, schemes in J. O'Toole and J. Dunn, *Pretending to Learn*, NSW Australia, Longman, 2002; N. Kitson and I. Spiby, *Drama 7–11*, London, Routledge, 1997.

9 For an example with older children where prejudice is carefully allowed to be articulated, responded to and discussed more openly, see Chapter 6 (3a, b).

10 See *The Uses of Enchantment*, Harmondsworth, Penguin, 1978.

11 J. Neelands '11/09 The Space in our Hearts', *Journal of National Drama*, Summer 2002.

Drama, English and citizenship

Drama, English and spirituality

'The Selfish Giant'

Context

This project is suitable for children between the ages of 6 and 9 and was developed with a class of six- and seven-year-olds in a voluntary aided Church of England school with a high percentage of children identified as having learning difficulties. It was planned as complementary to a science-based topic which concentrated upon plants and growth. The teacher was looking towards the drama to provide a spiritual dimension to the work. As gardens were a major contextual reference point within the science topic – the imaginative play area, for example, was set up as a garden centre – we agreed that Oscar Wilde's story of 'The Selfish Giant' would provide the foundation for the drama work.

Outline of the drama

The drama closely follows the original story line, which begins with a group of children playing happily in the giant's garden. One day, after an absence of seven years, the giant returns and banishes the children, declaring that he wants the garden entirely to himself. However, when spring eventually arrives, it remains winter within his garden until one morning he awakens to the sound of bird song and the sight of sunlight streaming in through his window. He looks out into his garden and sees that children have found their way back in to play there; and that where they are playing, winter has given way to spring. He realises how selfish he has been and declares that he will never be so again. He notices that winter remains in a corner of the garden where a little boy is crying beneath a tree. The giant runs to lift him on to one of its branches and immediately the snow melts and the tree blossoms into life. True to his word, from then on the giant allows the children into his garden to play but never sees the little boy again until one day when he is very old. This time he notices wounds in the palm of his hands and in his feet but the boy calms him with the message that these are the wounds of love. He invites the giant to come and play in his garden forever from that day forth. When the children come to the garden the next day they find the giant lying dead beneath the tree, covered in white blossom.

Learning intentions

1. To explore the themes of selfishness and redemption at the heart of the story 'The Selfish Giant'.

2. In English:
   - Listening, asking relevant questions, following instructions, responding to presentations, describing character, considering how mood and atmosphere contribute to performance.
   - Writing character profiles, letters in role and short poems.

3. In drama:
   - Exploring character and issues through a range of dramatic conventions including role play; hot-seating; tableau.
   - Creating and sustaining atmosphere through use of sound and movement.

4. In science:
   - Revising the conditions that enable green plants to grow.

5. In art:
   - Being introduced to famous works of art depicting gardens and the Christ child.
   - Painting flowers from observation.

Specific objectives

NLS	Y2/2: T1, 3, 6, 8, 9, 10, 14
NC Speaking and listening Key Stage 1	1a, b, c, d, e, f; 2a, b, c, d, e, f; 3a, b, c, d, e; 4a, b, c; 6a, b; 8c, d; 9a, b; 10a, b, c; 11a, b, c
Speaking, listening, drama objectives	Y2: 13, 14, 16, 18, 20
NC Science Key Stage 1	3a, b, c
NC Art Key Stage 1	1a; 2c; 4c

Resources

An old jacket to wear when in role as the giant; a drum and beater; a large bare twig; green and gold lametta or tinsel; a small doll; a sheet of white netting; recorded music (4b; 5a); digital camera and appropriate software; story of *Persephone*; green sugar paper; BBC hymn book; powder paints.

UNIT 1

(a) Presenting the pretext

Draw the outline of a large garden on a flipchart and sit the children in front of it. Ask them what they would like to have in this lovely big garden for it to be perfect for them to play in. Write in their suggestions. Tell them that the garden belongs to a giant who has been away for a long time.

(b) Mime work/dramatic play as individuals and in small groups

Ask the children to choose their favourite of these activities without telling anyone what it is. At your word, they go into space and mime playing there individually. After a minute or so, stop the children and negotiate with them where the various activities are in the space. This will allow you to group children according to where they want to play. When you re-start the activity, encourage children to talk and play with one another and to tour the garden at will. Interact with them yourself to encourage their imaginative engagement.

(c) Establishing the problem – the giant!

Gather the children together in front of the flipchart. Invite them to talk about the games they have been playing and the things they have particularly enjoyed doing in the garden. Then narrate how one day the giant returned and put up a sign. Uncover the sign prepared in advance on the flipchart 'Children Keep Out! Trespassers will be Prosecuted'. Ask children if anyone can read it and explain what it means. Then ask why they think the giant has put it up. You may wish to emphasise that they have been very careful with his garden, so that any fears he has of them damaging it are groundless. Further questions to ask are:
- Why do we think he has made the sign so big and written the letters in bright red?
- Could we say anything to the giant to persuade him to change his mind

and let us play? Could we bring him anything to show him that we are friendly?

Let children discuss and share their ideas about what these tokens of good will could be.

(d) Dramatic play in pairs

Tell children to work in pairs to make/buy/gather/write whatever small token they wish to present to the giant. Have them sit in a circle and ask a child to fetch a(n imaginary) sack from the corner of the garden. Briskly take it around each of the pairs and have them say what it is they are putting into it as they do so. Then ask for two volunteers to quietly place it in front of the giant's door. Ask for more volunteers to show you with their faces how pleased they think the giant will be when he sees the presents. Then ask them to watch quietly to see what happens when he answers the door.

(e) Teacher in role as the giant

Narrate how the giant came to the door and saw the sack but no sign of the children who were obviously hiding. Then, as the giant, talk in a grumpy voice and take out some of the actual presents the children put into it in the previous exercise. Be very ungrateful, throwing them back into the sack and then calling out to the children, wherever they are, that you are not interested in their presents. It is your garden, not theirs, and they are not welcome in it. Conclude by narrating: *And with that the giant slammed the door!*

(f) Hot-seating the giant

Tell the children that they are going to have a chance to interview the giant to find out what sort of character he really is. Prepare some questions then take on his role as they hot-seat you. Be grumpy, not frightening, true to the details of the book but prepared to embellish them according to what the children ask you.

(g) Sculpting the giant (1)

Model this activity with one of the children first, showing how to sculpt a partner into a statue. In pairs, children sculpt partners into the giant to embody his attitude in the story so far. Take photographs with the digital camera. Consider suitable adjectives together and write these down.

(h) Writing activity – character profile

Now that the children have seen and interviewed the giant, what do they know about him? Create a feather map with them to help organize what they have learned from the hot-seating (see Figure 4.1 for the map created by this class). Then read through it aloud, modelling how it can be used to create a character profile, e.g. *The Giant is very selfish. We used to play in his garden but now he keeps all of the children out of it. When we asked him why, he told us in a very grumpy voice that he wants it all to himself etc.*

Now ask the children to write their own profile for a child who is just about to move into the house next door to the giant's and who would like to know what he is like.

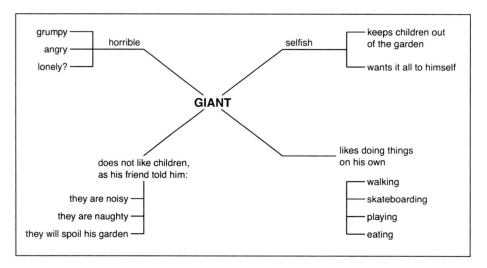

Figure 4.1 Character profile

(i) Stillness and reflection

Display one or two paintings of beautiful gardens, by Monet, for example, and encourage children to study them quietly for a minute or two while you play some soothing music.

UNIT 2

(a) Physical work – creating the barriers

Gather the children around you in front of the flipchart. Narrate: *Now the giant called in a company of builders and asked them what barriers they might construct to keep children from getting into his garden. What do you think they recommended to him?* Write down a list of what they suggest, e.g. railings; barbed wire fencing; brick walls with cut glass cemented to the top. Call for three volunteers and model how they can use their bodies to make one of these barriers, such as the railings. Then put children into groups of four or five and ask them to choose a different barrier and do the same.

(b) Vocal work – creating the warning signs

Tell children that each section of the wall had a sign on it designed to carry a terrifying warning for any child who might try to get through the barrier. Each group creates their own and then has to vocalise it in a way to match its meaning. You might work on one together first to demonstrate how to play with pitch, dynamic and tone.

(c) Whole class performance. Can a child break through the wall?

Each group must now incorporate the physical with the vocal work. When you are satisfied that each group is ready, explain to the class that they will present their work in turn as we see what happened when a small child tried to break into the garden. Take on this role and narrate how you tried to climb through each barrier in turn. Each time you approach a group they are to form and vocalise the warning on the wall whereupon, frightened, you run away to the next one.

(d) Sculpting the giant (2)

The children are to imagine the giant looking from his window as the small boy runs away. Working in pairs, they sculpt their partners to physicalise how he looks. View half the class at a time and gather adjectives or phrases from the children to describe his look, e.g. cross; proud; scowling. Write these down.

(e) Discussion/classroom display/reflection and stillness

Ask the class to think about the kind of things people say when they don't want to play with anyone or to share their things with them. Write these suggestions on separate cards and, with children's help, use them as bricks to build a wall on a display board. Read through the bricks together in suitably expressive voices. Ask children to read the wall again in silence for a few moments and to think about why such phrases are like an invisible wall that people sometimes build around themselves.

UNIT 3

(a) Create winter coming to the garden

Sit the children down in a circle and narrate: *The giant suddenly became very, very cold so he went back into the house and he heard more things that told him that winter had come to his garden. First he heard this.* Make the sound of wind with your voice – children are to copy you; then of the pitter-patter of rain (clicking finger and thumb); of rain falling more solidly (rubbing hands together); the thud of heavy rain (slapping hands against each thigh alternately); then the pounding of a storm (drumming feet on the floor). Now divide the circle into four. Give each group one of the sounds of rain to perform. All of them can make the sound of the wind. Tell them that you will help them create the storm together and then show what effect it had on the giant. Challenge them to watch and listen as well as be the storm. Build up the storm sound by sound and act out the giant being unhappy, lonely and frightened. End with the cry *'It's spoiling my beautiful garden. How can I make this terrible weather go away??'*

Ask children why they think winter has come to this garden and only this garden and why it won't go away.

(b) Create the dance of winter in the giant's garden

Present children with a large picture of a bare tree in winter. Talk about the different shapes they can see and list words such as spikey, twisted, thin, sharp, etc. Have them play with making these shapes with their fingers, hands and arms, then, individually and in space, with their bodies. Then, in groups of four or five, ask them to create shapes which provide these impressions of the bare trees in the giant's garden. Use a tambourine to help guide their movement in unison from side to side as the wind blows, then perform these to music. Then, as individuals, have children make sharp, frosty shapes and explore how they can use it to travel. Refer them to the phrases in the wall you created together (2e), asking them to choose one of these and to chant it in a suitable voice as they move through the space. At a given signal they are then to move into their groups and form their tree shapes. Practise this and perform it as a whole class to music.

(c) Sculpting the giant (3)

This time the children repeat the sculpting exercise to show the giant cold and alone in his wintry house.

(d) Writing – poetry

Refer children to cards that you have produced from the three lists of words that describe the giant in the three different moods. Using these and adding new words when necessary, show how some are of one, some of two, some of three syllables. The children help you create lines of poetry thus:

> *Bad, grumpy, miserable giant*
> *Cross, scowling, furious giant*
> *Sad, lonely, shivering giant*

Put children into their literacy groups and present them with blank cards on which to write more words appropriate to describing the different moods of the giant and help arrange them into various combinations of one, two and three syllables.
The class can practise reading these together with strong rhythms and to different dynamics, deciding which best match the different moods of the giant.

(e) ICT

Using some of the photographs you have been taking of the giant in his different moods, show children how to play with some of the effects of the software available on your computer, such as *Microsoft PhotoEditor*. For each line and its matching photo, ask them to choose an effect that goes with the intended mood. Then they can experiment and find a suitable font for the text. Use a selection of these to begin a wall display that will eventually show the giant's journey from selfishness through isolation into joy.

(e) Stillness and reflection

Play some music appropriate to the feel of winter. Ask children to close their eyes and to think of the giant in his house alone as it plays.

UNIT 4

(a) Physical game/warm-up

Have children move into and through the space. When you call 'Freeze' have them stop. Then they are to imagine that they are a wall. Each time you beat the drum a piece of them has been knocked down. On the third beat they fall to the floor. Play the game three times.

(b) Storytelling

Sit the children in a circle. Play some soothing music softly and story tell how the winter seemed to last forever but on one morning the giant awoke to the sound of birdsong. He saw sun streaming through his window and as he looked through it he saw that some children had indeed found a gap in his wall and were playing in the garden. All around where they played the sun shone and the trees were in blossom and the frost in the giant's heart melted as he realised how selfish he had been. In one corner of the garden, however, winter remained. There a small boy was crying because he could not climb into a tree. The giant felt so sorry for him that he ran down the stairs over to where he stood and gently lifted him onto a branch. It will help if you have a large twig and a small doll to enact this scene. The boy laughed and kissed the giant on the cheek and the last of the snow melted and the tree sprouted leaves immediately. Here you could drape a thin strip of green lametta or tinsel over the twig. The giant vowed that from now on all the children would play in his garden and he decided to knock down the walls straight away!

(c) Physical work – breaking down the walls

Children create their walls again. To the beat of a drum they have to gradually collapse, taking three beats to do so. If you have a large, plastic hammer, have a child perform the hammering and another child beat on the drum in time to it. Different children can take it in turns to knock down the different sections of the wall as you watch each group in turn.

(d) Dramatic play/teacher in role

Then everybody could play again!! Let the children play for a while then stop them for a second to explain how you will be coming into the garden as the giant to play with them. As you go round the different groups, ask the children how to play and make giant-like mistakes – pushing the swings too hard; jumping into the pool and emptying all of the water, etc. Each time apologise meekly and ask the children to teach you how to play gently.

(e) Creating a still image

Form the children into groups of three or four and place them in different parts of the garden. Ask them to create a **still image** of the giant playing with the children there. They must try to make it clear what they are playing and which one of them is the giant. Then ask them to add a caption that lets us know what it means to the giant, after all he's been through, to be playing with the children like this.

(f) Stillness and reflection

You might now read children the story of 'Persephone' and play them a few minutes of music appropriate to the feel of spring. Ask them to close their eyes and think of the giant playing happily with the children as they listen.

(g) Song 'Break Out'

This can be found in the BBC hymn book.

(h) Discussion/display work

Displace the bricks on your wall display to illustrate that the wall has collapsed. Place the outline of a bare tree behind it. Have seven or eight large green leaves cut out of sugar paper. Tell children that these leaves contain words and phrases that are the opposite of those in the wall and invite them to help you write in what they might be. Have children then place the leaves at different points on the branches.

(i) Role play and writing – providing information

The giant is now happy to work in his garden again, but the plants need a lot of care after the terrible, long winter they have suffered. As different groups spend their allocated time in the garden centre (imaginative play area), present them with letters from the giant asking for various pieces of advice and saying that he will call in later that day. Give them time to read and prepare, then either yourself, a teaching assistant or one of the children can take on the role of the giant. Later they can write a letter of reply to the giant. Use a feather map to help prepare their responses.

UNIT 5

(a) Storytelling and ritual: the end of the story

Sit the children in a circle and tell the end of the story. Again, appropriate musical accompaniment might be helpful. *The giant always looked out for the little boy but he never came again until one day when the giant was very old he dozed off and awoke to see him back by the tree that was now covered in gold and silver.* Show the children a small branch that you have decorated this way. *But on approaching him, the giant saw that the child had wounds in his hands and on his feet. The child calmed the giant by telling him that they were the wounds of love and said that, because the giant had let him play in his garden, he, the boy, was inviting him to play in his own garden for ever. When the children returned to the giant's garden the next morning they found him there, dead beneath the tree, covered in white blossom.* Place the jacket on the floor in the centre of the circle and cover it with the white netting to symbolise the giant. Place your golden branch carefully on a chair next to this. Explain that all of the children wanted to write a small message or give the giant something as a last thank you. In silence, children either write a message or draw a picture of their present and come back into the circle. One at a time they bring it into the circle and place it around him, saying what it is they have brought or reading their message aloud.

(b) Stillness and reflection

Now read the original story to the children.

(c) Discussion

This can be a good time to help the children articulate some of the symbolism of the story. What do we know of the little boy? Was there anything magical (or miraculous) about him? How is he like Jesus? Could he have been Jesus? Where would his garden be? Why was he inviting the giant up to heaven? What kind of a garden do you imagine it as? It is a good time to introduce the concept of redemption to the children, framing it within ideas of doing wrong, being sorry and being forgiven. Children might also be shown pictures of the Christ child, such as those painted by Raphael[1] and be asked to think in what ways he is like the little boy in the story.

(d) Complete display work

Children create two final images of the giant, joyful and at peace and write two final lines of poetry as in (3d) to complete the display of the giant's spiritual journey. These can be organised in a circle around the display of the fractured wall and the tree (4h).

(e) Art work

Around this display, tell children they are going to create the garden the giant has been invited to live in by painting tall, beautiful flowers. Bring some colourful flowers into class and discuss carefully with them what they can see, the shapes and shades of colour. Using powder paints, choose one of the flowers and demonstrate how you mix colours attempting to capture a particular shade in one of its petals. Let the children comment on your success. They can then paint their own versions of the flowers on large sheets of paper: after all, they must be big if the giant is to enjoy them!

Spiritual education: nurture and critique

There has been a long tradition of statutory provision for Religious Education in the UK, consolidated in the 1944 Education Act. By the time of the later 1988 Act, however, British society had changed in ways that made the legal requirement for a religious – and more specifically *Christian* – education more problematic. The power of organised religion had declined, secular liberal humanism was much stronger in political and educational circles and changes within the ethnic and cultural diversity of Britain meant that, for many schoolchildren, faiths other than Christianity were practised at home and in the community. Stating that schools were to have a responsibility for the *spiritual* and *moral* rather than the *religious* education of children consolidated what had become a growing consensus that left schools and teachers freer to interpret what a spiritual education might consist of.

Definitions of spirituality have, however, proved to be elusive, but there is general agreement over the areas a spiritual education will be concerned with. These include issues of profound significance that remain ultimately mysterious – the existence and nature of God, for example; or whether there is any fundamental purpose to human existence; whether there is any life after death. Complementary to such issues is the nature of spiritual experience itself – feelings of harmony, communion and deep, spiritual belonging for example. The fact that these issues and experiences have been traditionally rooted in religion does not of necessity make spirituality the prerogative of religious study alone. Artistic expression, for example, has often been culturally associated with religious experience, and since the Romantics, art, music, poetry and literature have commonly been regarded as sources of spiritual nourishment in themselves. Similarly, the study of science and mathematics can provide opportunities to inspire awe and wonder at the complexity and beauty of the natural world. Such a vision will tend to imply a cross-disciplinary approach to spiritual education, and this has, in fact, been the dominant model in UK schools since the 1990s. Andrew Wright has called this the 'inclusive' model for, not only does it reach across the subject disciplines, it also views spirituality as distinct from religious experience. Wright has defined its central premises as follows:

> It identifies a universal spiritual experience as the foundation and source of our search for life's meaning and purpose. Guided by feelings and emotions and our capacity for creativity, such spiritual experience is presented as a fundamental aspect of the human condition, transcending our ordinary everyday experience. (2000: 72)[2]

The inclusive approach to spiritual education therefore sees spiritual experience as more universal and hence more fundamental than religious, moral and rational experience. Such experiences, it argues – of awe and wonder when gazing at the stars on a clear night sky, for example, or of being profoundly moved by a piece of music – do not need any specific religious framing to be truly felt, because spirituality is not exclusive to religious believers. In the inclusive model, the central purpose of spiritual education is therefore to sensitise pupils' curiosity, imagination and intuition. In the words of Priestley, it aims 'to give people a greater reliance on the validity of their own inward and private experience' (quoted by Wright 2000: 74).

As a teacher, I might immediately wonder how I am supposed to know when such authentic experiences have happened. However, as has already been argued, an educational aim need not be dismissed out of hand simply because it is ephemeral in its nature and out of synch with current models of rational planning, visible learning objectives and targeted outcomes. There are more pressing criticisms of the inclusive model to consider.

First and foremost, the model privileges the private and the individual at the expense of communal and social experiences of spirituality, valuing autonomy above relationality; freedom over commitment. There is no reason to assume that, just because my inward, personal feelings are deep and authentic that they are of necessity benevolent. They could, for example, be deeply racist. In contrast to this, Hay (1998) has developed the concept of 'relational consciousness' from his own research into children's spirituality.[3] This he argues is a fundamental biological tendency that drives human spirituality, and he views modern individualism as a cultural rather than a natural phenomenon that works against it. He proposes a spiritual curriculum taught within 'a context of ritual, communal narrative . . . and social teaching which both focuses attention on and gives concrete expression to spiritual insight' (1998: 158). The fact is, of course, that many of these communal rituals and narratives are found within the contexts of traditional faith systems and values. The ideology of modern individualism that underlies the inclusive vision will tend to regard such faith systems suspiciously, filled as they are with culturally bound prejudices, inimical to the values of objective truth and individual choice. But the traditions to which these values belong are the reality of our histories. To ignore their stories as educators is to ignore the roots from which contemporary values have emerged. The freedom that the inclusive approach promotes is therefore one of rootlessness and vacuity. It is, to borrow the words of Alasdair MacIntyre 'the freedom of ghosts'.[4]

Closely associated with issues of communality and tradition are issues of language. As was argued in Chapter 2, language should not be seen as a transparent carrier of objective meanings but more as a conveyor of diverse cultural values whose expressions we seek to decipher rather than effortlessly absorb. The inclusive model tends to describe spiritual values in terms of universal human qualities, such as 'awareness, wonder, gratitude, hope, energy, gentleness, basic trust, self-acceptance' listed by Beck (1991) and Evans (1993).[5] Devoid of context, however, these qualities are emotive but relatively meaningless. Take self-acceptance and basic trust as just two examples. In what spiritual way do I 'accept' the fact that I am short-tempered, self-centred and prone to drinking too much alcohol at the weekend? Who am I meant to 'basically' trust? Must I include politicians and secondhand car salesmen in my list? It is obvious that such terms are far from unproblematic. If this is true of such seemingly warm and straightforward concepts, where spiritual and moral values appear to elide one into the other, how much more problematic are the more culturally specific spiritual concepts such as grace and redemption, to draw two from my own Roman Catholic upbringing. In the inclusive model, lists of universal spiritual values tend to emphasise those that sound cosy and comforting, avoiding the darker, more disturbing manifestations of spirituality. Martyrdom, for example, is celebrated within the annals of many faiths in ways that conflict with secular, liberal humanist values; and yet it continues to impose itself sharply on the contemporary world, shaping ideologically driven action in ways that affect children's as well as adults' lives.

To critique inclusive education in this way does not imply an outright rejection of its attempts to find spiritual values in secular contexts, nor does it imply a return to an exclusive educational agenda strictly boundaried by religious orthodoxies. But it does propose that critical reflection on spiritual values will never be possible without a grasp of their rational and emotive power and the public forms of discourse through which they are expressed. As these discourses have been historically and culturally framed in religious as well as philosophical terminology, Wright proposes twin functions for spiritual education: nurture and critique. In this way he believes it can work towards Freire's model of emancipatory education by enabling pupils 'to identify and articulate their own spiritual presuppositions . . . and to locate these in a broader map of society, history, culture and ideas' (2000: 132).

Nurture and critique through English and drama

In the light of the above commentary, an integrated approach through English and drama can be seen to afford particular contributions to a spiritual curriculum. The cultural uses of language and story are, as we have seen, at the heart of spiritual traditions, and it is through language, metaphor and stories that spiritual values and spiritual concepts enter the public domain. The capacity for literature, poetry and drama to address fundamental issues of ultimate concern and to 'move' people profoundly through their aesthetic qualities is commonly appreciated. We may not be able to force children into such an appreciation but we may well feel it worthwhile to nurture them into it by offering experiences that provide a space in which it might possibly happen. When we recall that spiritual concepts can only be grasped or critiqued by considering them in context, a further role for drama can be identified that draws upon its active, performative nature.

Both individually and communally, spirituality is expressed through the body as well as through language. Rituals of prayer, meditation and celebration work through specific patterns and styles of language and demand particular responses from the body. It is easy for us, given our cultural knowledge, to spot from their actions the person who has actually come to a cathedral to worship as distinct from the many tourists who have come to admire the architecture. This is because worship and other spiritual acts, both communal and individual, are performed. Such performances are not only an outward expression of the experience but also the means through which the experience is apprehended. When charismatic Christians sing, clap and dance, for example, it is as much a means to access the experience of joy as it is to publicly demonstrate it. This principle holds true away from organized religious practices. Meditation, for example, demands stillness, muscular as well as mental concentration and is enabled through adopting specific physical positions.

Such performances, culturally determined as they are, often make use, just as theatre does, of symbolic objects that are saturated in meaning. In a Catholic church, a statue is more than an artefact representing particular spiritual virtues as embodied in a saintly life. People will often light a candle in front of it or pause to pray. The pouring of water over a forehead during the sacrament of baptism symbolises the cleansing of the soul through the power of grace. In secular contexts, lucky charms, photographs, plants, all manner of objects can gain spiritual significance in people's lives and are sometimes the focus of personal rituals that are highly significant for the individuals who perform them.

We can now consider these points within the context of the proposed twin aims of nurture and critique. In order to nurture children into feeling, expressing and understanding spiritual values we must provide them with opportunities to experience them. In a church affiliated school, this may appear to be more straightforward than for a non-denominational state school. But drama, of course, operates within a fictional context. It is a way for children to explore and apprehend experience without actually undergoing it. Rituals, symbolic artefacts and other means through which spiritual values are expressed can be built carefully into drama work in ways that are intended to nurture children into *knowledge* rather than into *belief* – knowledge of their own and other people's spiritual values rather than a belief in a particular orthodox view.

Knowledge of this kind is a necessary premise to any form of critical reflection. As with critical literacy, critical spiritual knowledge has an emancipatory agenda inasmuch as it can help children understand how powerful forces operate upon them and not always in their own best interest. Drama can play a key educational function here because it is often through theatricality that spiritual experience is aroused. The story of the *Nine O'clock Service* is a salutary example.[6] The service was intended to appeal to young people and was the work of a religious group based in a Church of England parish in Sheffield, UK. It drew upon New Age religious tendencies and included coloured lighting, dancing and rave music and ran from 1988 until 1995, when sexual scandal discredited its minister and chief organizer, Chris Brain. The appeal of the service lay in its theatricality, and it was highly successful in bringing young people into the church. We must remember, too, that the Nazis knew how to use the theatricality of the Nuremberg Rallies in order to arouse powerful communal emotions, no less spiritual for the darkness at their heart. Understanding how drama works, how its effects are managed, can alert children to the ways in which powerful spiritual feelings can be provoked within them for manipulative purposes.

Spiritual education within the scheme 'The Selfish Giant'

As this scheme is intended for young children, the spiritual emphasis is on nurture rather than critique. In other words, it attempts to involve them in an expression of certain spiritual values, to feel and appreciate their significance and know more about them. Much of the scheme chimes readily with the aims of the inclusive model, as its attempts to provide space for spiritual experience are largely structured around values that are general and secular. However, rather than gloss over the specifically Christian elements inherent to the story, the scheme attempts to highlight them where they occur. The intention here is not to indoctrinate children but to provide them with knowledge. Whether children are Christian or not, if they are not taught to recognize these values and their symbolic representations, any future critical engagement with Christianity will be either ill-informed or incomprehensible. The model provided in this scheme for illuminating spiritual values can be applied to traditions other than Christianity.

Wilde's story is, at base, a Christian parable. The child is Jesus, the wounds are those he received on the cross; the garden into which he leads the giant is paradise. The tree is a powerful symbol of the cross. When the giant places the little boy in its branches, they immediately blossom into life, symbolic of the everlasting life that Christians believe Christ's sacrifice on the cross has promised. His heavenly glory is then reflected in the final appearance of the tree. 'Its branches were all golden and silver fruit hung down from them.' The tale is sometimes seen as a moral fable to encourage sharing, but it is more accurately viewed as a tale of redemption. The giant has to atone for his selfishness through the harsh purgatory of winter before he can learn to be sorry for his sin. Through his love of the Christ child he learns the Christian virtue of Charity, and as a result finds happiness in this life and the next.

The vision of Christianity the story projects is, however, one very much tinged with socialist values. The Jesus we are presented with is the one who grew up anonymously in a village and who later told the rich man, if not to cast aside his possessions entirely, then at least to share them if he wanted to enter the kingdom of heaven. The giant – aristocrat, landowner – can only achieve happiness when he shares his land with the children, or the common people. This state of common ownership is portrayed as natural throughout the tale; birds and flowers all side against the giant's law of private property, only making an appearance in his garden when the children are there. In this way Wilde's story performs its function as a parable, embodying Christian values in a way that critiques their absence in a late Victorian society which prided itself on its Christian virtues. It is insufficient to wait for the afterlife, Wilde is saying; we must try to create a heaven on earth. For a contemporary audience of young children, this critique is still relevant, presenting the Christian message as supportive of a particular vision that promotes principles of social justice.

The scheme attempts to follow closely the rhythms and values of the story in an embodied, enacted form. Because of the power of the story, the spiritual values can be argued to be pervasive throughout the scheme, but specific activities are meant to serve particular purposes in nurturing spiritual knowledge through experience, enactment, writing and reflection.

Modelling and embodying spiritual values in concrete form

- The children not only witness the giant at specific moments of the story, they also enact him. These moments embody him at the different stages of his journey through selfishness, isolation, contrition, joy and redemption. Work (in 5d, e) then encourages children to make overall sense of what the spiritual meaning of this journey has been. When I storytell the ending, I do so actively, adopting the role of the giant, kneeling and bowing before where the boy is standing, joining my hands in prayer, then stretching one out towards him in awe. Such actions permit children to share in the spiritual power of the moment through culturally specific enactments.

- The walls that the children create (2a, b, c) are primarily social metaphors of rejection and selfishness but, as the drama develops, their meaning gains a spiritual dimension within the giant's journey to redemption. This is reinforced by the words of the song (4g) and by the writing and display activities (2e, 4h).

- Through their dramatic play children create the garden as a place of joy (1b). Later, through their dance (3b), it becomes a place of cold and hostility. Later again, (4d, e, f) it is a place of joy once more, not only for them, but for the giant, too. The art work that completes the project emphasises the link between gardens and paradise that spans the Jewish, Christian and Islamic faiths.

- The display of the giant's journey, created over time and completed in (5d), is a further activity intended to help the children understand the concept of redemption articulated in (5c).

Making the spiritual values visible through symbolic objects

- When telling the story, I like to use a twig or small branch that suggests the shape of the cross and coloured lametta to help children visualise the symbolisms of life and glory (5a). This is meant to help establish a connection with Christian symbolism, as are the historical illustrations of the Christ child.

- The white netting over the giant's jacket represents the white blossom but also has resonances of spiritual purity in Christianity. In Hinduism, of course, white is the colour of death. It is always important to ask children what they read into such a use of symbol rather than tell them what you meant it to signify.

Performing the values through ritual

In the most obvious use of ritual in this scheme (5a), the children thank the giant and say goodbye. Children can be very good at sustaining the right mood here in something that resembles a funeral rite. In this way they can experience the emotive power of such communal acts without feeling any real sense of grief. Their words, in effect, constitute a communal prayer and you can help model the solemnity of the occasion to help them find the correct register. Of course, if a child has recently lost a relative then this ritual might be uncomfortable for them, and individual teachers must always follow their own professional judgements here.

Reflecting on the values through stillness

Each unit contains a moment of stillness and reflection, with some form of stimulus and focus to provoke children's thinking. The stimulus generally takes the form of music, poetry or art for reasons explored above. It is important that these moments are short and not accompanied by any pious homily or moralising so as to avoid the feel of a school assembly!

Articulating the values through discussion and writing

All too often we limit the language we use in our teaching to its more transparent forms, giving and seeking definitions, explanations, etc. More expressive language, as typified in the language of poetry and fiction, can be among the best ways to help children apprehend and give voice to values and experience. In this scheme, (5c) is the only activity that is intended to help children make these values transparent. In (2e), (3d, e) and (4h) they are approached laterally, in expressive ways. The power of a good story, however, lies in its suggestiveness, its resonance, and we can never determine what lasting impressions it will leave on children. We need not as teachers be apologetic about this; rather we should seek ways of maximising its impact, and drama can be among the most powerful of our options.

Notes

1 Examples can be easily found on a Google image search.
2 A. Wright, *Spirituality and Education*, London, RoutledgeFalmer, 2000.
3 D. Hay, *The Spirit of the Child*, London, Fount Paperbacks, 1998.
4 A. MacIntyre, *After Virtue*, London, Duckworth, 1981: 127.
5 C. Beck, *Better Schools*, London, Falmer, 1991; D. Evans, *Spirituality and Human Nature*, New York, SUNY Press, 1993.
6 See http://members.tripod.com/~nineoclockservice

Drama, English and ICT

'The Forbidden Planet' (a scheme based on Shakespeare's The Tempest)

Context

This project is suitable for children between the ages of 8 and 12. It was devised for a Year 4 class (aged 8 to 9) in a school where 90 per cent of the children were British South Asian, either first or second generation, most of whom spoke a language other than English at home. The work was designed to follow on from a

Learning intentions

1. To explore some key themes from *The Tempest* centring upon issues of power within family, gender and colonial contexts.
2. In English:
   - Critical reading and interpretation of written texts;
   - Questioning characters, speculating upon motive, offering advice, challenging interpretations;
   - Script writing, report writing, reflective writing, writing a measured argument.
3. In drama:
   - Interpreting character through careful consideration of language, gesture and costume;
   - Responding to and making appropriate use of symbolic objects;
   - Representing characters through gesture, language and symbolic objects;
   - Planning and presenting small improvisations;
   - Working from script.
4. In ICT:
   - Finding and downloading information;
   - Locating, reading and replying to email;
   - Processing digital imagery;
   - Creating a whole class powerpoint display.

science-based topic on space and to explore creative and integrated ways of using ICT for both teaching and learning. All the activities took place in the classroom, with the desks and chairs cleared for the drama work. It ran as a block, taking over 75 per cent of the timetable for a week. The activities are presented in an order which suggests natural divisions between drama, literacy, ICT and art sessions. As with all the projects in this book, these are presented as guides rather than blueprints. This project is particularly well suited to team teaching.

Preparation

In order to teach this project, some preparatory work is needed. If you are not well acquainted with the play, you will need to read it, or see a production of it and also read a children's version of it, such as Leon Garfield's.[1] Although this scheme is a simplified and changed version, it is important that you have a knowledge of the plot and of the relationships between the key characters, as the scheme attempts to remain true to some basic themes of the play. In addition, you will need to set up an email account and prepare and practise the powerpoint presentation which is an integral part of the first unit.

Outline of the plot

The children take on the role of space explorers, with the teacher as their captain, Antonio. They have been sent on a mission to investigate a strange radio signal from a distant planet. What they do not yet know is that their captain and his admiral, Alonzo, conspired to abandon Antonio's brother, Prospero, there some twelve years earlier with his baby daughter, Miranda. Both men gained promotion as a result of his disappearance. An added complication is that Alonzo's own son, Ferdinand, is a member of the ship's crew. Exiled on the planet, Prospero has meanwhile managed to increase enormously the powers contained in his 'Book of Knowledge' by coming into the possession of a magic staff that he took from Caliban's mother, Sycorax, before using it to imprison her in a tree. It is through these powers that he has lured the space ship to the planet and conjured up a meteor storm to make it crash.

In the aftermath of the crash, Antonio discovers that Ferdinand has disappeared. Ordering the crew to stay on board, he leaves the ship. The crew discover from his personal file clues to his guilty secret and, disobeying his orders, explore the planet. First they find the caves in which each of the characters live and then the truth about the relationships between them and the missing members of the crew, Ferdinand and Antonio. They learn how harshly Caliban is being treated and that this is because one day he had tried to kiss Miranda. When she had slapped him in response, he had thumped her. They learn, too, that Miranda has just met Ferdinand and immediately fallen in love with him but that Prospero disapproves of this. In Shakespeare's play, Prospero is being darkly playful, testing Ferdinand's love, but in this version there is no play-acting, he does not want his daughter to marry his enemy's son.

Caliban then tries to lure the crew into a bargain. If they can capture Prospero's staff, they will secure his power. If they then deliver Prospero and his daughter over to him as his prisoners, he will show them how to use the staff to escape the planet. Prospero, however, is aware of his treachery and intervenes, offering his own bargain to the crew. The drama ends with certain moral ambiguities that the children may or may not be sympathetic with.

Although this may sound quite complex for a classroom drama, it is organized in simple stages that the teacher can easily manage.

UNIT 1

(a) Pretext – reading and responding to email

An email arrives on the class computer from Admiral Alonzo asking for recruits to fly on a space mission and inviting applications for particular jobs. His own son, Ferdinand, will be on board so he is looking for experienced and responsible applicants, who are requested to complete a personal file by way of an application, enclosed as an attachment (see Figure 5.2). Help children share the jobs out and have them help you complete your personal file before writing their own. Try to make the jobs as equitable and as non-gender specific as possible – scientists; medical officers; store managers; engineers; navigators, etc. Have sufficient jobs so that children will work in groups of four or five. Digital photographs of each of the children can be taken and they can be shown how to load them onto their files. Later that week Admiral Alonzo sends a second email. All applications have been accepted apart from your own as your physical and mental profile suggests you are unfit for space travel.

(b) Opening activity – dramatic play

The children are to work in their groups at their jobs. Discuss what they will be doing and introduce the item of costume you will wear when in role as Captain Antonio. Tour in role, ask questions, respond to enquiries and set tasks. Then call the groups together to practise the crash landing procedure, should the sign WARNING! flash on the computer.

(c) Teacher and computer in role!

As Captain Antonio, assemble the crew in front of the screen or interactive whiteboard. Introduce them to the ship's computer, giving it a name (we called ours Manjit). Inform them of the purpose of this secret mission. Admiral Alonzo has sent you to investigate a radio signal detected from a planet in Space District 299, which you are now approaching. However, it is no longer detectable so you are going to abort the mission. At this point, the ship's computer begins to contradict you (see Figure 5.1). The dramatic purpose of the subsequent interplay is to begin to cast suspicion on Antonio.

You can dialogue with the computer by preparing a series of slides that constitute answers to questions you put to the computer. You ask a question, then surreptitiously click on the mouse for the computer to give its response. For example,

ANTONIO: Good morning Manjit.
COMPUTER: Good morning captain.
ANTONIO: Manjit, there is evidently no further reception of the radio signal, so we shall return to earth.
COMPUTER: Wrong captain. Human ears cannot detect it but I can.

If when creating the slide show you use the *crawl from left* option in the *effects* button, the writing on each slide will appear a letter at a time, giving a visual representation of speech happening through time.

You can also download images of forest, vegetation, water, etc. to make slides that visually contradict Antonio when he asserts that there can be no life on the planet. Antonio ignores all of this and says that the ship will return to earth anyway, at which point the next slide declares WARNING! METEOR STORM! the signal for the crew to get into their crash landing positions and the end of this section of the dialogue.

Figure 5.1 Dialoguing with the computer

(d) Narration and dramatic play

Suddenly the WARNING sign flashes on the computer. Dispatch the crew to their crash landing positions and narrate them through the crash. In their groups, they can then examine their particular areas for damage. Anyone injured can report to the medical officers.

(e) Whole class

Reassemble the class in front of the computer. Listen to each report then consult her. She informs you (via two or three powerpoint slides, as in Figure 5.1) that all guns have been mysteriously neutralised, that there is a hole in the starboard side of the ship and that Petty Officer Ferdinand is missing. As Antonio, you are shaken by this news. Inform the crew that you will leave the ship and search for him and give strict orders that no-one is to follow you.

(f) Finding Antonio's personal file

No longer in role as Antonio but in a **shadow role**, able to talk to the class as crew members, discuss Captain Antonio's behaviour with the class. In what ways is he acting suspiciously? Yet why does Admiral Alonzo seem to have such faith in him? Has any of the crew seen his personal file? Can anyone find it on the computer, do they think? Choose likely volunteers to attempt this and talk you through the process. Once downloaded, display it and ask the class/crew to read it for information that might provide us with clues to explain Antonio's suspicious behaviour (see Figure 5.2)

(g) Writing reports

Children write a report for the ship's log on the crash and provide details of damage to their area of the ship.

STAR SHIP 'THE TEMPEST'

PERSONAL FILE OF CREW MEMBER

NAME: Antonio   PHOTOGRAPH:

(Insert your photograph
here)

POSITION OF RESPONSIBILITY:

Captain of the star ship 'Tempest'

PREVIOUS EXPERIENCE OF SPACE EXPLORATION:

Many years of service in admiral's fleet. Served as vice captain to his brother, Prospero, on ill-fated mission twelve years ago to Space district 299. Brother about to be promoted to Admiral but went missing with young daughter while exploring planet. Alonzo appointed Admiral in his place. Antonio then promoted to rank of captain.

SPECIAL QUALITIES:

Very determined. Will do what it takes to get his way. Very ambitious. Wants to be among the highest ranking officers in the star fleet.

This crew member has been approved by ADMIRAL ALONZO, commander of the space exploration fleet.

Figure 5.2 Antonio's personal file

UNIT 2

(a) Reading and responding to email

An email is received from Alonzo asking his son to reply to him immediately. Debate with the crew how you should respond in the light of the information gleaned from Antonio's personal file. Should we tell him the truth? Do we delay and write back pretending to be Ferdinand? Compose a reply together.

(b) Dramatic play/game

In your shadow role, revise with the children what they learned about the planet from the interplay between Antonio and Manjit in the previous unit. Present the crew with the latest report from Manjit (projected onto the screen, if possible). It tells how Antonio is in a nearby forest but that strange noises are adversely affecting radio reception. However, she has detected evidence of life in three caves nearby. Ask the crew if they are prepared to disobey Antonio and go and investigate these caves. Play the game **Through the Magic Forest** then divide the crew into three equal teams.

(c) Using clues to create characters

If you have adult support, the three teams can work simultaneously on these tasks. The adult/teacher simply needs to lead the questioning and respond to the children's suggestions. The three caves can either be set up in advance or the teacher can narrate their creation, e.g. *As the crew arrived, they found that this cave contained a rope (place the rope in the space); an empty wine bottle with a note in it* etc. These are the caves of the three principle characters – Prospero, Miranda and Caliban. Each contains objects and a piece of writing, clues to the person who lives there and their relationships with the other two. Possible samples of writing are included as Fig 5.3. The objects should include:

- *Prospero*: things to denote both scientist and magician – test tubes; rock samples; science books; a white coat; a silver globe or crystal ball; his huge 'Book of Knowledge'; his magic staff (a stick wrapped in silver foil!).
- *Miranda*: things to denote a girl who is both child and adolescent – a necklace of shells; a chain of flowers; coloured silks; beads/simple jewellery; a doll.
- *Caliban*: a rope; an empty wine bottle; bits of rubbish – fishbones, apple cores; a candle stub; an old jacket; one or two logs for furniture; an old cracked mug.

The children/crew should use these clues to speculate and then sculpt either the adult or a volunteer into the shape of the imagined character. Concentrating on the writing, they should then suggest how it should be read – voice, intonation, etc. The adult can respond to and follow their ideas and then model this reading. The sculpted character and the reading can be integrated to present a performance to each of the other groups to show what they have discovered.

Caliban

These ropes! They burn my wrists! Prospero, I curse you and hate you! You and your simpering daughter. You came to my planet and befriended me. I revealed the good things of the planet to you, not knowing that you would capture its powers and make them work for you. Now you control everything in my world. You insult the memory of my mother Sycorax by calling her a filthy witch and have made me your slave, to live and work in misery. Whoever shall read this letter I write – help set me free from such a wicked master! Help me kill him and his daughter and recover the land that right-fully belongs to me. Then shall Caliban forever be in your debt.

Miranda

Oh, how handsome he is! That slim young man whom I met wandering through the forest, dazed. He told me his name is Ferdinand and I told him that mine is Miranda. He spoke to me so sweetly and smiled so warmly. I have no memories of any other company save for my dear, sweet father and the hideous creature called Caliban. How strange it is that I used to feel sorry for Caliban, despite my father's warnings. But ever since that awful day when he attacked me, how glad I am that my father keeps him bound and tied to a stake. And yet Ferdinand is no Caliban, so why does father seem to hate him so? Why is he punishing him and breaking his daughter's heart in the process?

Prospero

My dearest Miranda. Do not weep for those who were on board the ship. Yes, it was I who caused the storm but I used my magic staff to make sure that no-one would be hurt when the ship crashed. You see, I lured the ship here and with it my enemy, whom once I called a brother. And you must forgive me if I punish the son of the accursed Admiral who conspired with him to abandon us both here all those years ago. Surely you see that I cannot let you become the friend of your father's sworn enemy? Be patient, my daughter for soon my revenge will be complete and we shall no longer have to remain alone on this planet with that vile, hideous beast, Caliban.

Figure 5.3

(d) Sculpt your partner/game

In pairs, children take turns to sculpt one another into one of the three characters, emulating what they have just seen. Then play the game **Through the Magic Forest** again, as they return to the ship. Here Manjit provides us with a written version of a radio message relayed by Captain Antonio during our absence.

> ANTONIO: (crackles of radio) This is Captain Antonio reporting to the starship *Tempest* (strange, tinkling sounds can be heard). My compass seems to be faulty and I . . . I appear to be lost in the forest (more strange sounds, this time deeper, rumbling). No-one must leave the ship. Repeat! No-one must leave the ship (radio crackles, more strange sounds). I . . . I . . . so sleepy . . . (his voice sounds increasingly tired and grows fainter) so . . . sleepy . . . (radio crackles and goes dead).

The crew read through the message and speculate as to what has happened when, suddenly, the teacher in role asks for quiet and moves quietly to the door of the ship to listen. Yes, you are sure, there are footsteps approaching the ship! End the drama at this point.

(e) Literacy/writing

Looking again at the writing in Figure 5.3, children speculate as to the history of conflict and closeness between the three characters. In groups, children draw up lists of questions they would like to ask one of them, with different groups working on different characters.

(f) Working from script

Using the transcript in (2d), children create a live or recorded version of this message, working on intonation and sound effects, choosing appropriate instruments.

Figure 5.4 Miranda's cave

(g) Making models of the three caves

Using a variety of materials and boxes, children in groups work to create a model of one of the characters' caves. Children can then digitally photograph them and download them for Manjit to store (see example, Figure 5.4).

UNIT 3

(a) Reading and responding to email

An email has arrived entitled 'For Captain Antonio – strictly confidential'. Debate with the children/crew whether you should read it or not. Its content will depend upon your reply to (2a). Decide with the children how to reply. Now could be a time to tell him what you suspect and to ask some hard questions.

(b) Meeting and hot-seating the characters

The footsteps approaching the ship belonged to the three characters. The children have just five minutes to hot-seat the teacher in role as each of the characters in turn. Each should have a prop or item of costume to designate their role – coat, staff and spell book for Prospero; scruffy jacket and woolly hat for Caliban; a chain of flowers for Miranda. The teacher and/or teaching assistants can use these throughout the rest of the drama to signal which they are when in role. The key points that should emerge refer to the joint histories of the characters and their feelings towards one another and should be the same as in the original play.

(c) Working and performing in pairs

From the information they have now received in (3b), children in pairs are offered different key incidents that have been referred to from the past and are asked to recreate them as short snippets of action with a few lines of dialogue. They are:

- Antonio reporting to Alonzo after Prospero's abandonment on the planet;
- The immediate aftermath of Caliban's attack on Miranda;
- Prospero's treatment of Caliban;
- Ferdinand and Prospero's first meeting.

They are encouraged to decide with which character their sympathies lie and to make sure that their presentations reflect this. Contrasting and conflicting sympathies are to be welcomed.

(d) Script writing

Children use this work to script short scenes with stage directions as to tone of voice and gesture. You can introduce this as a whole class literacy session, using a different scene as a model – for example, the first meeting between

Miranda and Ferdinand. Have the actual words written/projected onto the board/screen in advance. Ask children for ideas as to how each line should be spoken, actively modelling their suggestions. They should look at you and listen carefully and suggest what the stage directions as to tone of voice, facial expression and gesture ought to be. You can then model how to write these in. Children can be grouped according to which scene they worked on with their partners in (3c).

UNIT 4

(a) Reading and responding to a message

There is no email this morning but a message has been left. It is unsigned and is inviting the crew to a meeting to help them escape from the planet. From the style the crew will suspect that it is from Caliban. Play **Through the Magic Forest** or a similar game to get to the meeting.

(b) Dramatic play and forum theatre

In role as Caliban, tell the children that you are willing to help them escape. First, however, they will need to neutralise Prospero's power by stealing his staff, bringing him and Miranda to you in your cave. Do not relent on this. If the crew wish to know what you will do with them, refuse to tell them. Then challenge them to come up with a good plan to steal the staff. Put them in groups to plan and practise this and, rather than have them describe their plans to you, say that you, Caliban, will play the part of Prospero for them to test out their plans. You know all his ways of science and his magic powers. In each case, you will find it relatively easy to thwart their plans, playfully pointing out their shortcomings.

(c) Narration

When you feel it is appropriate, use a drum to signal silence and narrate how, at that moment, the voice of Prospero boomed out in anger *'Caliban! Did you think I would be ignorant of your treachery? You have betrayed me for the last time!' But Caliban, whimpering in terror, tried to blame the crew. 'No, master, it wasn't me, it was these people. They tried to trick me into helping you but I wouldn't agree.' 'Silence!' roared Prospero. 'I shall deal with you later. And as for the rest of you, I will help you leave the planet but only on two conditions.' And Prospero told the crew what these conditions were . . .*

(d) Small group performances

Divide the children into small groups and ask them what they think the two conditions might have been. Ask them to agree an exact wording and to practise speaking them together in the voice and physical stance of Prospero. Each group performs this as you present them with the staff.

(e) Writing: Caliban's character

Children discuss how they feel towards Caliban and are encouraged to express ambivalence. In guided writing groups, they can write points under headings such as 'We felt sorry for Caliban when . . .' and 'We didn't like Caliban when . . .' and/or other headings they might suggest. More able children can be encouraged to write in paragraphs rather than bullet points.

UNIT 5

(a) Reading and responding to email

Two emails arrive. In the first, Alonzo confesses his involvement in the abandonment of Prospero and expresses his remorse. The second is from Prospero, informing the crew of his two conditions to fix their ship: they must take him and Miranda with them and offer him advice as to how he should resolve the dilemmas he now faces with his brother Antonio; Miranda and Ferdinand; and with Caliban. First he would like them to question Antonio. Discuss the implications of these messages before moving on.

(b) Hot-seating Antonio

Prospero has had Antonio under a trance since his last radio message. This will ensure that he tells the truth. Prospero would like the crew to question him as to why he did such a terrible deed and then advise whether he should be forgiven or not. Frame some of the questions together before taking the hot seat as Antonio. Be the jealous younger brother who thought he would never have the opportunity to prove himself if he didn't get Prospero out of the way. At the conclusion, out of role, allow children in small groups to decide what Prospero should do. Rather than tell you, they can present their ideas as a 'collective Prospero' as in (4d) announcing their decision as you approach each in turn. As Antonio, reply to each differently according to what each group says to you.

(c) Game: Prospero's maze

This is a version of the game **The Wizard and the Maze** and can be contextualised as a troubled dream of Prospero's.

(d) Forum theatre

We can now see the main source of his worries. Miranda is unhappy. As Miranda, sit in the hot seat and tell the children that you have had a row with your father over Ferdinand. You want to marry him but he won't let you as he is the son of his enemy. You feel it is wrong to take your revenge on a son for something the father may have done in the past. You feel that you should be given a choice over these matters yourself and have warned your father that he cannot keep you locked up forever. The children can tell you what they think and can give you advice as Miranda on what to say to your father in order to persuade him to let you marry Ferdinand. The scene can then be replayed as forum theatre, yourself in the role of Prospero and different children in role as Miranda.

(e) Sculpting images

Children sculpt two volunteers into images of Ferdinand and Miranda that could possibly conclude their story. Encourage different possibilities, so that 'happy' and 'sad' endings are considered should there be disagreement. Help the children to consider gesture and facial expression to make the images as clear as possible. It is also important to ask children to tell you why they think it will end this way. Children will enjoy sculpting you and a teaching assistant into these possibilities. Alternatively, you can put children into fours and ask them to sculpt two contrasting endings, one happy, one sad.

(f) Ritualised action and final still image

As Prospero, ask the crew to attend to their stations and place your Book of Knowledge in the centre of the space. Produce the staff and ask crew members from each group to take it in turn, placing it first on the book, then over the damaged part of their station. If they are silent and concentrate, tell them, the staff will do its work. Let them then play for a few minutes preparing for take-off before narrating how Caliban's voice could suddenly be heard screaming from outside the ship, asking not to be abandoned alone forever. As Prospero, ask the crew quickly, what should you do. Listen to what they have to say then inform them that Caliban's punishment is to be abandoned.

Stop the action, and ask for volunteers to sculpt you or a child, or to show themselves as they think he looks in this final image. Create a **line of allegiance** to show where their sympathies lie in the fate of Caliban.

(g) Concluding the drama

What should Prospero do with his staff? Ask the children out of role then mime what he did do, 'breaking' it over your knee and ejecting it out into space. Discuss why they think he might have done this.

(h) Presenting a written argument

Children consider who received Prospero's justice, who his forgiveness, who his revenge and what they feel about each decision. They write on one of these.

(i) Creating a whole class powerpoint display

The ship's log needs to contain a visual and written record of the whole adventure, as experienced by the crew. Compose a list with the children of the key incidents that should be included in it. Small groups or pairs of children can then create these images, be photographed, programme them as powerpoint slides and add suitable captions. The display makes an excellent contribution to a class assembly or parents' evening. (See Figure 5.5.)

ICT in education: heavenly visions and images of dystopia

Computers are incredibly fast, accurate and stupid. Humans are incredibly slow, inaccurate and brilliant. Together they are powerful beyond imagination. (Albert Einstein)

From a personal perspective, none of the changes in primary education that the UK has witnessed since 1997 seems to have been quite so marked as the rise in significance of Information and Communications Technology (ICT). In terms of resources alone, UK primary schools have been transformed. Computer suites, as well as banks of computers in classrooms, are now common, as is access for children and staff to the internet, to laptops, digital projectors, interactive whiteboards, digital cameras and camcorders. Such a vast input of resourcing has been unprecedented in my professional career and anything similar is unlikely to happen in the foreseeable future. So what impact is this revolution meant to have on education? What is the ideological vision that underlies such a huge investment?

At a national conference in January 2002, the then UK Secretary of State for Education and Skills, Estelle Morris, presented her vision for the classroom of the future. Miles Tandy has written a vivid account of this, in particular of the video that accompanied her speech.[2] Technology is everywhere, the video tells us, 'from plasma screens to lap-tops and palm-tops, headsets and electronic links to facilitate self-directed learning'. The technology is intended to offer children of all abilities 'the chance to learn at their own pace alongside one another, studying individually or in groups' (2003, p. 235). He then quotes at some length a remarkable section from her speech.

> I think ICT is our DNA – it's our internal combustion engine. It is the trigger that can bring about a revolution in how we teach and how pupils learn, and that's why it's not just one more change – it's not just one more thing, it's not just one more Government announcement – it's not one more thing that fades out with time when teachers think that something better has come on the market. It's actually the thing that can change, and change for ever, how we teach children and how teachers do their job. (Morris, cited in Inman *et al.*: 2003: 236)

ICT is a revolutionary force, she is telling us, that will change economic and cultural lives as fundamentally as the Industrial Revolution once did. Yet she goes beyond this, expressing an almost theological faith in its utopian potential. The acronym ICT is transformed into the equivalent of DNA, suggesting an underlying vision of the information revolution as parallel to the discovery of the secret of life itself, the ultimate source of power. Crack the secret of ICT, she is saying, harness its potential, and we have discovered the answer to our most fundamental educational challenges.

Of course such utopian visions of possible futures promised by technology are not new and are, indeed, characteristic of the kind of modernist thinking that has driven educational reform in the UK since the invention of the National Curriculum in 1988. But there is something particularly potent about the promise of utopia as it relates to ICT. Tim Jordan has analysed the nature of what he terms the 'virtual imaginary – the collective imagination of cyberspace' (1999: 180).[3] This imaginary, he tells us, is a cultural construct, a set of beliefs, hopes, fears and myths that are held, proposed or fostered by those who use, promote and theorise ICT. At its heart is the belief that 'everything is made up of information and can be turned into information' (p. 181), a belief that has been stimulated by enterprises such as the human genome project, established to crack the code of DNA. As computers and the internet are essentially hyper-efficient information processors, the metaphor of life as information that this project embodied is extremely potent for those, including Secretaries of State for Education, who foster utopian dreams for the future based upon the potency of ICT. 'Information', writes Jordan, 'is dreamt of as the magic component of the new age that is dawning at the beginning of the third millennium' (p. 193).

> At its most rhapsodic, the heavenly imaginary of cyberspace offers both immortality and godhood to humans through the translation of life into information held in cyberspace. (p. 180)

Expressed in these mythic terms, the Secretary of State's utopian vision can be understood as influenced by a current imaginary that promises dreams of power that, unsurprisingly, have great appeal to a politician. For imaginaries 'are in a constant state of almost becoming real'.

> [They] offer hopes and fears that often do not appear as hopes and fears but as real projects just one or two steps away from completion. (p. 183)

And lest this argument seem somewhat exaggerated, it is sobering to relate these mythic dreams of god-like power to the quote from Einstein at the start of this section, one that I heard at a recent head teachers' conference. Concentrate less on its humanist vision and more on the vision of power *'beyond imagination'* that is heralded here by the father of nuclear physics.

However, like all imaginaries that emanate from dreams of technological power and progress, there is a dystopian as well as a utopian side to the vision, a Frankenstein's monster for every Eddystone Lighthouse, a fear for every hope, a hell for every heaven. In this case, we need only view such dreams of power through an Orwellian lens to understand the fears of what Jordan describes as 'a Superpanopticon of total surveillance' (p. 180). The amount of personal information that computers are able to hold in vast databanks, electronic tagging, the insertion of chips into people's bodies, such possibilities make ICT a perfect tool for social and political control. Of course, Morris's vision is distant from this, but both utopian and dystopian visions are united by their dreams of power. They are opposite sides of the same coin. However benign the language and serene the imagined future expressed by Estelle Morris, it is sobering to position her speech within the context of educational reform over the last ten years, where increasing control over teachers, pupils and the curriculum have been central to the reforming agenda.

Neil Postman also expresses a dystopian vision of computer technology drawn from his own perspective as an educationist and cultural commentator.[4] His argument is that every new technology brings with it an underpinning ideology that is often hostile to progressive social change. Like any technology, the computer has invaded our thought processes and changed the way we view the world and relate to it.

> The computer [he writes] redefines humans as 'information processors' and nature itself as information to be processed. . . . It subordinates the claims of our nature, our biology, our emotions, our spirituality. The computer claims sovereignty over the whole range of human experience, and supports its claim by showing that it 'thinks' better than we can. (1992: 111)

Postman shares a similar understanding to those who hold a utopian vision – that computer technology demands a redefinition of how humans relate to information. For him, however, unlike Einstein, this redefinition is profoundly inimical to our humanity.

> We move to the proposition that humans are little else but machines and, finally, that human beings are machines. And then, inevitably, . . . to the proposition that machines are human beings. (p. 112)

The danger here lies in the pre-eminence then given to the computer in educational terms. Computers can access and process information at remarkable speeds and hence become a strong cultural force that fosters a limited vision of what knowledge consists of and hence of what education should concentrate upon – namely speedy and efficient information processing. Yet Postman argues, as Schön has done,[5] that none of our most pressing problems are the result of inadequate information processing. World hunger, family violence and rising street crime will not be solved through vast quantities of information alone. Similarly, as Tandy points out (Inman *et al.* 2003: 238), computer generated knowledge is a poor metaphor for the personal, social and moral needs of school-children. To present a vision of ICT as *the* answer to our educational challenges is vastly to overstate its case. Such advocates need to learn what Paul Goodman has termed 'technological modesty'; that is, 'having a sense of the whole and not claiming or obtruding more than a particular function warrants' (cited by Postman 1992: 119).

ICT and education: culture as well as skills

Whatever our own personal stance is with regard to the place of ICT in education, we cannot remain ignorant of the vast changes it is bringing to the lives of young people. Computers affect the way we communicate, play, shop and find things out, but their cultural effects go far deeper than this. New technologies are having a profound effect on how we think about ourselves and how we relate to the world; and these impact upon and are in turn shaped by other contemporary cultural forces. As an example, let us briefly look at one aspect of our humanity that ICT impinges upon, that of our social identity.

The presentation of self on-line is fluid and mutable. In chat rooms, through email accounts and in special interest groups, a female can pose as male, a disabled person as able-bodied, a fifteen-year-old as someone much older. Jordan shows through a number of case studies the complex, ambiguous though arguably democratic effects that such fluidity of identity can bring to people's relationships and sense of self (1999: 59–99). Of course, the media almost invariably present this in a negative light, emphasising, in particular, the opportunities such mutability affords paedophiles to 'groom' potential victims. John Carroll, however, stresses the significance that the metaphor of 'morphing' has had on the lives of young people.[6] They, he argues, have already absorbed its implications, which have led them 'increasingly to inhabit the world of surface, conveyed by the computer screen and enacted on the internet' (2002: 137).

> This new metaphor allows them to reject the idea of the unitary self, one career path, one job for life, one definition of self, one gender division, . . . one notion of the body. (ibid.)

Unlike Postman, he does not view these effects in a negative light but sees computer technology as enabling, promoting a way of situating oneself in the world that chimes readily with recent cultural as well as economic theory. This is a vision of the self as 'culturally constructed', in which identities are not fixed and unchangeable but better understood as 'necessary fictions'. So career path, birth location, religious affiliation, even gender are seen as less deterministic than they once were, as identities are more fluid and open to reinvention in the contemporary, globalised world. Using Giddens's term (1991),[7] Carroll suggests that identity has become more of a 'reflexive project' than a predetermined, fixed state (2002: 137).

If this is indeed the case, then the opportunities afforded by computer technology for young people to experiment with their identities, playfully creating and revising their biographical narratives and their styles of self-presentation, can be seen as fulfilling a pressing but liberating cultural need. Such identity play is potentially educational in a cultural rather than a skills-based sense. As such, it can be seen to relate directly to the kinds of identity play that are afforded by drama. It is to investigate this relationship that I now turn; how drama can contribute a critical, cultural and creative dimension to what otherwise might be viewed solely in terms of skills acquisition, with all the ignorance that implies of the ideological baggage that is carried in an ICT curriculum. First of all, I would like to consider what these two unlikely curriculum partners, drama and ICT, might share as processes.

Drama and ICT: comparing their educational processes

For performance purposes, developments in ICT open up new opportunities for drama, just as they do with other subjects. Computerised lighting, digital video cameras such as the *digital blue movie creator*,[8] the potential for the use of multimedia, all provide new possibilities for dramatic performance. The internet, too, opens up opportunities for research in ways similar to those it affords to other subject disciplines and can be used to inform specific drama projects. Beyond this, however, there are interesting comparisons to be made between the *processes* of drama and ICT, informative as to how the one can complement the other.

- As media of communication, both drama and ICT are able to make flexible use of words, images and sound and are hence subjects that demand competence in, and can be used to promote, multiple literacies.

- In terms of curriculum planning, both are often regarded as cross-curricular processes as well as subject-specific disciplines.

- ICT has strong performative uses beyond the obvious deployment of computerised lighting etc. Powerpoint, for example, is essentially a performative medium, though it is generally used to support performances in 'real life' contexts – job interviews, business presentations, conference speeches and the like. It can, however, be used in fictional contexts and, more interestingly perhaps, its performative potential can be dissociated from normal social contexts to be used creatively, as in (1c) of the scheme outlined in this chapter.

- There are deep differences between traditional dramatic narrative and the kind of narrative typical of a computer game. The latter relies upon a series of spectacles and sensations that follow in a rapid but simple sequential form, whereas the former is structurally far more complex, working through theme and characterisation, from equilibrium, to crisis, to a new form of equilibrium (see Carroll 2002: 134). Nevertheless, both drama and ICT, in the forms of participatory drama and computer games, can be said to mediate interactive forms of fictional play that follow a narrative pattern.

- Both drama and ICT enable different types of identity play.

- Digital photography, through readily available software packages such as *Microsoft PhotoEditor*, provides opportunities for a different form of identity play, enabling radical experimentation with visual representational imagery of all kinds, including of the self.

- The power of computers to retrieve and manipulate information in ways that far outstrip our own brains continues to fascinate us, a fascination that science fiction has exploited in the creation of cyborgs, or the fusion of man with machine. Films such as *Robocop, Blade Runner, Terminator* and *AI* explore this concept. Computers themselves have also been portrayed as having personalities, both seriously, as in *2001: A Space Odyssey*, and comically, as in the British TV series *Red Dwarf*. Thus computers already exist as *characters* rather than just as properties within popular drama and hence within the popular imagination.

Critically and culturally engaging with ICT through drama

Postman's pessimistic vision of the educational effects of ICT is itself ideologically positioned. In the final chapter of his book, he argues a particular vision of liberal education intended to counter the nefarious effects of computer technology on our humanity. This education should foster the best of human values that can be drawn from our cultural heritage. This idea, that education should above all be concerned with the transmission of 'the best that has been thought and said', has a long tradition and can be traced back to Matthew Arnold and the middle of the nineteenth century. A school inspector as well as a prolific writer, Arnold, like Postman, feared the dehumanising potential generated by the technological advances of his own era. He proposed a vision of education in which the cultural heritage of literature and drama, most typically enshrined in classic works such as the plays of Shakespeare, should counter their influence. Both Arnold and Postman, therefore, position culture and technology, arts and sciences, as binary opposites, the former as humanising, the latter as destructive of our humanity. Carroll's vision is more inclusive and optimistic. He sees those who criticise the cultural and educational effects of ICT as perpetuating an outmoded vision of a divide between high and low culture. Such a vision regards the dramas of popular film, which thrive on new technologies, as vastly inferior to the drama enshrined in our cultural heritage. This kind of binary thinking, he says, 'positions educated people as "sensitively attuned" to high culture drama or alternatively sees less educated people as "mindlessly enslaved" by low culture entertainment' (2002: 130).

If such a vision had motivated this project based on *The Tempest*, then Shakespeare would have been viewed as a rectifying curative, a humanising force in the face of a dehumanising, technically driven curriculum. His text would have remained sacred, his language and plot untampered with. In beginning from a position that noted complementary similarities between the processes of drama and ICT, however, the project actively attempted to bring them together. In this way, the cultural and technological possibilities of ICT were intended to deepen and embellish the drama while the contextual clarity, complexity of theme and symbolic potential of the drama were meant to add a cultural and critical dimension to the use of ICT. So how, exactly?

The emails that precede and accompany each of the Units have a particular function in advancing the plot, but they also allow children critically to interpret and play with identities. Similar to an avatar on the internet, Alonzo only exists in this drama on-line. Although his communications are brief, children are called upon actively to interpret, respond to and read the subtext of what he writes. In (2a) they write something they think he will want to read as a reply; in (3a) they respond with questions and accusations in a register that takes into account his position of authority; in (5a) they judge from his writing whether his remorse is sincere or not. All of this could be done through letters rather than email, but the cultural reality of email can provoke further, pertinent discussion. How do we recognize who someone is when they email us? Is it possible for someone to lie about who they are in chat rooms and email? Children will know quite well that this is possible because they will probably be very happy to accept the challenge of replying to Alonzo as Ferdinand or Antonio in (2a). What problems or dangers can that pose for us? Such critical questioning could also be applied to (1f) when the children download and read Antonio's personal file, although more general discussion of ethical issues concerning the uses of personal databases will be probably more accessible to older children. Lest the transgressive nature of these activities worry you, we need to remember that the overall reasons for the crew's actions here are for a greater, moral good.

The work with the emails, then, can be seen as complementary to the kinds of identity play and character exploration that is integral to the rest of the drama work, but how both drama and ICT help us 'morph' identity is further explored with the use of the digital camera. In the two images in Figure 5.5 we see examples of how children represented Caliban (in 5i) at different moments in the story. The images combine bodily representation with an added layer of spectacle made instantly possible by the application of digital software. It is illustrative of how two different approaches to identity play complement one another. The drama here provided the deep play, the story, the relationships, the fictional context that made a dramatic representation of Caliban possible. The photo editing software added surprising, surface, sensational effects, characteristic of computer games, striking in its visual power and other-worldly textures. A major delight for the children was to see their bodily images transformed in this way, particularly when they were enlarged through a digital projector. Such striking visual imagery is made instantly possible through ICT, bringing previously highly skilled, technical tasks within the reach of children. Rather than regarding such potential as culturally dehumanising, there is surely a strong argument to welcome it as democratising.

The children incorporated these images into a powerpoint display that was intended to archive the story in the ship's computer. But as with any representation of events, this exercise could be presented with a particular perspective or bias in mind. Prospero's selection of events and how they should be portrayed could be very different from one of the crew members, for example. The fact that images are seldom if ever ideologically neutral can be actively explored in this way.

The significance of the cyborg in popular culture has already been signalled, and the fact that our ship's computer has a name that denotes culture and gender, can apparently hear and is able to contradict the captain provides a good context for children to explore some interesting questions. Is Manjit alive? Is she really female? In what ways is she female? Could a computer be alive? What can she do better than humans, and what can't she do? A particularly interesting question (1c) is: 'Why did we trust her and not Antonio?' That can lead into a consideration of other situations where we might trust a computer more than a human being and vice versa. In this way we can playfully provoke a critical awareness of important philosophical issues at the heart of the developing relationship between human beings and computers.

Finally, let us return to Shakespeare. It is commonplace to refer to his genius in universalist terms, to regard his plays as speaking across time and across cultures, with different generations discovering the pressing concerns of their times reflected in all their complexity in his work. It occurred to me after the initial running of this project how Prospero did, perhaps, embody many of the questions raised at the beginning of this section, questions to do with the dreams and limitations of a particular type of power based upon an ability to process information at magical speeds. I originally used certain of the planet's rocks as the source of his power. This was intended to be symbolic of the planet's natural resources that Prospero's colonial technology was able to exploit. However, in exchanging this symbol for that of a large Book of Knowledge, whose power is processed by a magic staff, we move closer not only to Shakespeare but also to something symbolic of the particular dreams of power that pilot the utopian imaginary described by Jordan and resonant in the speech of Estelle Morris. It is significant that Jordan, when describing the utopian imaginary of information technology, refers to it as 'the magic component of the new age that is dawning at the beginning of the third millennium' (1999: 193). Oh brave new world, indeed, where the age old dreams of magic and the superhuman powers it can bestow upon us are as persistent as ever.

Power is a central theme in this drama and the issues are firmly centred upon the actions of Prospero: the power of a father over his daughter, a master over his servant, a coloniser over his land. The impressive way in which the children were able to engage with these complex issues is analysed in the final chapter. But if we dwell here on the nature and limits of Prospero's power, there are some interesting parallels to the nature and limits of the educational and cultural power of ICT. Prospero is able to use his power in coercive ways. He can use it to control nature (he creates the meteor storm), to control technology (he repairs the ship), to monitor behaviour (he knows when Caliban is trying secretly to betray him). What he can't use it for is to resolve the problems that, in many ways, matter most to him – the treachery of his brother and his servant and the contrary wishes of his daughter. His power does not and cannot extend to controlling the human heart. Here a different kind of knowledge is needed from that which can be processed from his Book, one that requires active meaning-making rather than information-processing, that aspires to wisdom rather than correctness, that grapples with concepts such as freedom, revenge and forgiveness (5f). Prospero's desire to throw away his staff at the end of the drama is ambiguous. We can read it as a recognition of these limitations, as a fear that whoever should inherit its power might not understand them, or as a mixture of both. In this way I muse that this particular Prospero finally attains, in symbolic form, an understanding of 'technological modesty'. Let us hope that those who dream utopian dreams of the promise of ICT manage to do the same.

Figure 5.5(a) Caliban feeling smug

Figure 5.5(b) Caliban abandoned

Notes

1 L. Garfield, *Shakespeare's Stories*, London, Gollancz, 1985.
2 In S. Inman, M. Buck and M. Tandy (eds), *Enhancing Personal, Social and Health Education*, London, RoutledgeFalmer, 2003.
3 T. Jordan, *Cyberpower*, London, Routledge, 1999.
4 N. Postman, *Technopoly: The Surrender of Culture to Technology*, New York, Vintage Books, 1992.
5 See D. Schön, *Educating the Reflective Practitioner*, San Francisco, Jossey Bass, 1983.
6 J. Carroll, 'Digital Drama: A Snapshot of Evolving Forms', *Drama and Learning: Melbourne Studies in Education, vol. 43 no. 2*, Victoria, Australia, Arena, 2002.
7 A. Giddens, *Modernity and Self-identity*, Cambridge, Polity Press, 1991.
8 See www.playdigitalblue.com

Drama, English and creativity
Blodin the Beast

Context

This project is suitable for children in upper primary and lower secondary years. It was devised for a class of nine- to ten-year-olds in a town school judged to have serious weaknesses and in which the underachievement of boys had been identified as a particular issue. The project was designed as a cross-curricular arts topic, including art, music and dance, steered by the work in drama and English. It was designed as a week-long topic, taking up approximately 65 per cent of the curriculum time, with some further time being set aside in the following week to complete art work and to prepare for a short performance. The story needs to be presented to the children in five episodes as the element of suspense is important throughout.

The story

Blodin the Beast, written by Michael Morpurgo and illustrated by Christina Balit, is a tale with many biblical echoes set in a mythical Middle-Eastern setting.[1] Blodin is a huge beast who drinks oil, breathes fire and enslaves entire populations. When the story opens, there is only one village left standing. The villagers all wish to surrender to Blodin and only the wise old man, Shanga, and a young boy, Hosea, refuse. Shanga has his life's work to complete, a carpet into which he has woven 'all the good in the world' and whose powers, he tells Hosea, are capable of defeating Blodin. Blodin burns the village and sleeps. While he does so, Hosea sets off alone on his journey, having to brave the dangers of the mountains, the forest and the desert. He carries with him Shanga's carpet, which also acts as a map to lead him to a land of peace and plenty. Having crossed the desert, he rests and dreams that Blodin awakens but that Shanga confronts and defies him. 'You may think yourself the strongest, but you are not. You may think you have conquered the world but you have not. Up in the mountains is a small boy and he is stronger than you.' Hosea dreams that Shanga is burned by Blodin and, as he awakens, he realises that Blodin is in pursuit of him. He flees and reaches the river as Blodin's shadow looms over him. A small voice in his head has been guiding him all along and now it tells him to trust the carpet and to float across the river on it. As he does so, Blodin plunges in after him, breathing his fire around him but Hosea reaches the far shore in safety as the waters of the river wash Blodin away. Beyond the shore, there are meadows and cornfields. Men and women are working together and children are laughing. He has reached the land of peace and plenty and Blodin is no more.

The story is a secular, postmodern myth, combining echoes of David and Goliath, Moses crossing the Red Sea and reaching the Promised Land, more than a hint of *Star Wars* and a very special magic carpet that recalls the *Arabian Nights*. All of these elements combine to create a powerful narrative that contains some of the ambivalence of myth. Take the words of Shanga to Blodin, quoted in the last paragraph, and apply them to the current political situation in the Middle East. Who do you identify as Blodin? The opening illustration shows hordes of slaves working in Blodin's oilfields, providing a strong symbolic image of multinational exploitation of the developing world. The beast itself looks metallic, drinks oil and breathes fire, an arch polluter in a hitherto unspoilt land. The final page is a utopian representation of an agricultural paradise, where third world peoples are happy, far away from the ravages of the globalised industrial pollution wreaked by Blodin. Such a portrayal of a mythical, unspoilt orient, where the

Learning intentions

1. To create the material for a performance based upon the story *Blodin the Beast.*

2. In English:
   - To discuss and critically reflect upon issues relating to the symbolic meanings of the story;
   - To read closely and select essential phrases and vocabulary from key sections of the text;
   - To write script, poetry and for persuasion.

3. To create performance drama through:
   - Sound collage;
   - Physical and vocal chorus work;
   - Dance/movement;
   - The use of abstract materials – cloth, canes, flags;
   - ICT sound files.

4. In art
   - To create a whole class rug with fabric crayons;
   - To create a sculpture of Blodin from various scrap materials.

Specific objectives[2]

NLS	Y5/1: T5, 8, 9, 10, 16, 18, 19, 20
NC Speaking and listening Key Stage 2	1b, c, e, f; 2a, b, c, e; 3a, b, c, d, e; 4a, b, c, d; 8a, b, c; 9a, c; 10a, b, c; 11a, b, c
Speaking, listening, drama objectives	Y5: 48; 51; 54; 55; 57
NC Art Key Stage 2	2c; 4a, b; 5b, c.

people would be happy to forgo modernisation, is, of course, as much a myth as the tale itself. So perhaps there is an element of naivety in its more obvious symbolic meanings. Feminists might also remark upon the unselfconsciously male nature of the tale. It is a classic hero quest in the masculine tradition – a lone, rather than a group endeavour, a boy's rite of passage into manhood, an older man bestowing the mantle of wisdom upon him. The only females in the tale express panic and a willingness to become Blodin's slaves, or, in the final picture, are seen to be happily carrying sheaves of corn, and even Hosea's carpet, while the men and boys look on. Nevertheless, it remains a powerful tale, a myth for our times, beautifully written and illustrated. The project attempts to harness its strengths and also to build in some exercises intended to help children critically engage with what I see as its more problematic aspects.

UNIT 1

(a) Introducing the story

There is a double page illustration before the tale begins showing Hosea and Shanga facing one another. Hosea looks distinctly androgynous. Question children about the two characters, including their gender, without telling them anything other than Hosea's name. Then read the first two pages of the story. Page 1 introduces Blodin and his apparent indestructibility, page 2 the villagers and their panic. It ends with their pleas to Shanga to surrender to Blodin and with his enigmatic refusal: 'I will stay. I have my weaving to do.' I accompanied all of my readings throughout the project with the music 'Kashmir' from the album *Symphonic Led Zeppelin*.

(b) Creating the Chant of the Slaves

Read the first paragraph one phrase at a time, placing great emphasis on the rhythm of the language. Have the class repeat each phrase. Then ask children to choose or adapt phrases from the page that tell us what Blodin did, e.g. stalked the land; drank only oil; breathed only fire. These can be playfully worked into a chant, e.g. Blodin the Beast/stalked the land; Blodin the Beast/drank only oil, etc.

(c) Group movement work: creating the beast

Ask the class to study the text and the picture for clues as to how Blodin might move. List these words, then put children in groups of five and ask them to create their own Blodin that can move in a controlled manner. The list of words is to influence their choice of movement. Give a structural challenge to the shape of the beast, e.g. it must have three distinct levels to it; children must be physically linked in different ways, etc. Alternatively, provide them with a choice of materials – cloth, netting, paper sacks, bamboo poles, etc. – and ask children to create their beast with the help of any they find useful. Here they will need more time to play with the materials and experiment before making decisions. When ready, each group can perform individually to the music.

(d) Physicalising and speaking text: the chorus of villagers

Turn to the second page of the book, read through it again and ask children to tell you how many sentences are spoken by the villagers (there are seven). Choose the first of these, 'He is coming, he is coming!' and read it in a dull, flat voice, asking children if that is how they think the villagers uttered these words. Respond to their suggestions and model a much more expressive delivery, adding facial expression and gesture, perhaps pointing in the direction of where Blodin could be. Now put children into groups of four or five, giving each group one of the villagers' sentences. Explain that they are to work out a way of performing this together, clearly expressing the emotions of the villagers through their bodies as well as their words. When these are ready for performance, hold a cloth over your arm and reply to each as Shanga with the words 'I will stay, I have my weaving to do.' Ask each group to watch the group that follows them very closely. After the performance, each group is to decide upon two things they particularly liked about the following group's performance and share them with the class.

(e) Teacher and class in role: what is Shanga weaving?

Put the class in role as villagers and ask if anyone has any idea of what Shanga is weaving. We know he is wise but what is he doing? Encourage the children to think of different possibilities and question them seriously on each. Conclude this discussion by drawing three or four questions that the villagers might like to ask Shanga, then take on his role. As Shanga, avoid answering their questions directly and throw a lot of what they ask back at them. *'Why do you think I am weaving a fake monster? Do you really think such a thing could deceive Blodin? How?'* etc. You can say that the weaving is your life's work and that you hope it may destroy Blodin but that it will need the help of someone young and brave. Are any of them brave enough . . .?

(f) Writing script

Refer to (1d) and remind children how the tone of voice and use of gesture were central to a good performance of their lines of dialogue. Illustrate with the children's help how to write a script of the first two or three lines of (1d), concentrating upon appropriate stage directions. In guided writing groups, the children can now be asked to write a script based upon the villagers' dialogue with Shanga in (1e). It will not be exact, tell them, and the differences between versions will be interesting. Set them the target of about ten lines of dialogue, with no more than two sentences in any one line. Higher ability children can be given the challenge of attempting to write in what they feel is the style of the author.

UNIT 2

(a) Reading the next section of the story (pp. 3–5)

Read the next three pages of the story in which Shanga explains what he is weaving to Hosea (p. 3); Blodin destroys the last village by fire and sets his slaves digging in its valley for oil (p. 4); and Hosea sets out on his quest (p. 5).

(b) Physical/movement work – the village in flames

As a warm-up, ask children to move in space, individually. On the word 'freeze' they are to stretch upwards and outwards in a sequence of symmetrical and asymmetrical shapes. Have them experiment with the direction of stretches, exploring different positions and balances. Bring the class together and have them study and describe the shapes of the buildings on page 4. Then, in groups of three, ask them to make one of these buildings from their bodies. It must be on at least two levels and have a tower. Emphasise the importance of balance, taut stretches and eye focus. Once these are created, view half at a time and ask children to help you organise them in space to create the village. Now bring the class together and brainstorm words that describe the movement of flames as they take hold then engulf the buildings. As individuals, have children explore the movements these words suggest. Back in their groups of three, they can work out a way in which to show their building slowly catching alight then being in flames. You can choreograph this by breaking up one of the groups and having the three children wave silk flags of red, yellow and orange over different groups in turn, then over the whole village, performed to appropriate music such as Holst's 'Mars'.

(c) ICT: creating the voice of Blodin by making a sound file

Have children list as many verbs associated with fire as they can think of – sizzle, fry, burn, scorch, grill, toast, etc. In groups of three, ask them to select from them to make a phrase that Blodin might gleefully say to one of his victims, e.g. 'I will scorch you!' 'Sizzle, fry, burn!' Ask them to say it in as menacing a way as possible then show them how to record it as a sound file on *Microsoft Sound Recorder*, standard software on school computers. The recording needs to be done in silence and with children working in small groups. However, once recorded, children do not need absolute quiet to play with the editing possibilities and dramatically alter their recording. Effects will allow them easily to amplify the sound; play the file at half speed (brilliant for Blodin!); play it in reverse (even better!); mix it with another file so that there are two or more phrases layered together. The final files, when played back with the volume turned up, can be highly effective and thrilling for the children.

(d) Poetry: 'In my carpet I will weave . . .'

The Kit Wright poem 'The Magic Box' is an excellent model for this poem.[3] The poem is a wish list for impossible or elusive things of beauty or desire that the poet would like to keep in a magic box. Each stanza appeals to different senses. Discuss these aspects of the poem, examining how the poet has structured the work. Then guided writing groups can produce their own stanzas, with each child producing and refining a specific line. Children may like to compose their own individual poems from the ideas the class produces, as in the following example, where the child imagined himself as Hosea.

> *In my carpet I will weave*
> *A gleaming shark of metallic blue,*
> *The sweet tickling taste of a rainbow,*
> *The shining light of a panther's eye.*

In my carpet I will weave
A smile from my best friend when I'm sad
A precious moment with my teddy late at night
The splash as I dive under the turquoise to the bottom of the river.

I will ride on the vast waves
With the enormous beast hot on my tail,
Then reach my destination
With Blodin swallowed by the crashing waters.
(Dan, aged 9)

Figure 6.1 Shanga's carpet

(e) Artwork: making Shanga's carpet

Each child is provided with a square of fabric and, using fabric crayons, is to make an illustration of one of the lines they contributed to the poem. When these are completed, they can be sewn together to create Shanga's carpet, containing the class's idea of all the goodness in the world.

UNIT 3

(a) Exploring gender issues in role

Explain to children that a friend of Hosea wants to talk to them, and take on the role of Hardgit, a girl who has always been his closest friend until now. Suddenly Hosea is going off on his own, telling you that you can't go with him as it is no job for a girl. Why do they think he is saying that? In the discussion, you can tell children, should they ask, that you have always been able to run faster than him, have always beaten him at arm wrestling, have always been the one to take risks, etc. After a few minutes ask them if they will talk to Hosea for you and see if they can persuade him to take you with him. As Hosea, be resistant and provocative. It is you, not she, who has been asked; besides, girls don't do this kind of thing, they are not as strong and should stay at home, doing domestic tasks like weaving. Look at the famous stories, it's boys who defeat monsters, not girls, etc.

(b) Letter writing

Tell children that they are to decide personally whether Hosea should let Hardgit accompany him or not. They are not to let anyone know what their decision is. If yes, they should write to Hosea telling him why he ought to let her come; if no, they are to write as Hosea to Hardgit, carefully explaining the reasons for his decision. This writing should be done privately and in silence. Give children ten minutes to complete it. What individuals have written can provoke further discussion.

(c) Reading the next section of the story (pp. 6–8)

This covers each of the three stages of Hosea's journey – over the mountains (p. 6), through the forest (p. 7) and across the desert (p. 8).

(d) Physical/movement work: Hosea's journey

As a warm-up, have children move individually through space, freezing in shapes that are suggested by the words you call out. Choose your words from aspects of the journey – mountain, eagle, creeper, sand dune, etc. With each, challenge children to think beyond the obvious, to dare to be different, by saying things like *Now give me a different kind of mountain, one that isn't symmetrical; now another where you are not standing upright*, etc.

The class is now to work on representing Hosea's journey. If you have classroom support, this is best done in three groups, each led by an adult, each concentrating on a different stage of the journey. If you have no support, you may think it best to concentrate on just one stage of the journey with the whole class.

Have the children look at the page concerned and say that we are going to concentrate on what Hosea can see, hear, feel and smell during this part of the journey. Make a mind map with them (see Figure 6.2). Encourage them to expand the language in the examples they give you, e.g. *He can smell the flowers, you say. What word might we use for the smell of flowers? Do you think it's a faint smell? So what kind of smell is it? What kind of flowers grow in a tropical forest?* In this way, the example becomes 'the heavy perfume of exotic flowers'. Write two or three similar examples for each of the senses, then put children into groups of two or three, depending on how many you are working with. Each group is given one of the phrases and they must work out a way of saying the phrase together and then create a movement motif to accompany it.

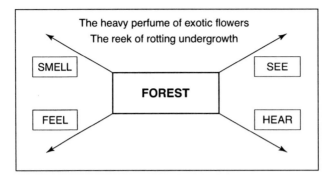

The heavy perfume of exotic flowers
The reek of rotting undergrowth

SMELL

SEE

FOREST

FEEL

HEAR

Figure 6.2

When these are ready for performance, take on the role of Hosea. Children are to remain frozen in their shapes until you pass them. While you walk around them they are to perform, stopping when you walk away. Children can then help you choreograph this, suggesting where certain groups ought to be positioned if they are to be best seen by an audience. You can also experiment with having the performances of two or three groups overlapping.

(e) Landscape poetry

Children can use this work as a basis for landscape poetry. This can also act as a script to record the performance, if children imagine it as a map of the performance, putting the phrase in the correct part of the page, using appropriate colour and font size to indicate how it was spoken (see Figure 2.6 in Chapter 2).

UNIT 4

(a) Reading the next section of the story (pp. 9–11)

Here we see how Shanga stands up to Blodin but is destroyed by him (p. 9); how Blodin pursues Hosea to the river (p. 10); how Hosea escapes across the river, which washes Blodin away (p. 11).

(b) Choral work: portraying Blodin's pursuit of Hosea

Study page 10 with the children and tell them that you are going to use phrases from this page to convey the growing menace of Blodin's pursuit of Hosea. Look at the first paragraph together.

> *He woke, and it was morning. But this morning the sun did not rise as*
> *it should. Instead, thick black fog was rolling in towards him across*
> *the desert.*
> *'Blodin!' he whispered. 'Blodin the beast has woken.'*

Have children choose the phrases that suggest menace and encourage them to strip them down to their minimum, e.g. *sun did not rise; thick black fog; the beast has woken.*

Now choose one of these and model how you can experiment with the pitch and dynamic of your voice to emphasise the menace, elongating vowels, emphasising specific consonants, etc. Ask children how different effects suggest menace and have them copy you. Turning to the rest of the page, have them talk in groups to find other menacing phrases, then list their suggestions. Share these out and have children working in threes to produce similarly evocative readings. These can be performed by you acting as conductor, bringing in different groups at different times, layering phrases together as in (3d). You can encourage the chanting to get louder as Blodin approaches.

(c) Working with flags: Blodin is defeated by all the good in the world

For this work, you need flags made of 1.5-metre lengths of very light, blue and white silk cloth, stapled to a length of bamboo, enough for one in three of your class. Read page 11 and sit children in a circle, showing them a flag and demonstrating how you can wave it carefully. Ask them what the cloth might represent from this section of the story. If some think the river and others the carpet, ask if it can be both at once. In groups of three, set children the challenge of swaying their flag carefully and in unison. Now ask them to recall their poems (2d) in which they wrote about the goodness in the world that was woven into Shanga's carpet. Choosing phrases that they contributed to the poem, ask children to work out ways in which their group can chant them as they wave their flag. Perform them in sequence, layering two or three together as in (3d).

(d) Discussion and poster campaign: Blodin is dead but his friends live on . . .

This section is intended to help children engage with the symbolic meanings of Blodin. Tell children that, although Blodin is dead, there are things in the present world that he would consider as his friends – those things that drink oil, breathe fire and smoke and destroy or harm land and people. Ask them to consider whom these friends of Blodin might be and why. Warfare and environmental pollution are obvious candidates. Map their ideas on the board. Then discuss possible slogans and images that they could use in a poster campaign to warn people to beware the friends of Blodin and the havoc they are wreaking. Make the posters and display them around the classroom.

UNIT 5

(a) Read and study the final page (p. 12)

Read the final page of the book and study the picture of the land of plenty and peace. Ask children to consider how this world is different from the world they inhabit then list the differences they note, e.g. we have cars, they have carts; we have engines, they use horse or people power; we have shops, they grow their own food, etc.

(b) Teacher in role: will we reject the friends of Blodin?

Now take on the role of Hosea. Congratulate them on their poster campaign. It has long concerned you that, although Blodin is dead, his friends live on and are causing similar damage. You are pleased that they have recognised the danger. Are they now prepared to take the final step to destroy his influence forever? It is simple – turn the world they live in into a world like the land of peace and plenty. Put aside their cars and walk; close all the factories and live with simple tools; abandon the shopping malls and grow and make all we need. We don't need electricity or gas or oil. We can light camp fires, sing and tell one another stories in the evening rather than watch television, etc. Of course, it will not take long for Hosea to realise that the children are quite reluctant to do all of these things, so ask them why, don't they realise that they don't need these material goods? Can't they see that they are playing into the hands of Blodin's friends? Look at the posters they have made! Surely they know this??

(c) Line of allegiance: what world do we prefer?

Have children create a line of allegiance according to which of the lands they would prefer to live in, that of peace and plenty or their own, Blodin-friendly land. Call them back together and discuss where they placed themselves and why and, if necessary, ask them to recreate the line and allow them to shift their positions if their opinion has changed.

(d) Discussion and reflective writing

In what ways are the friends of Blodin, listed in (4d), beastly? Which are we prepared to get rid of? As for the others, how can we tame them, making them less beastly, so that the world and its people suffer less from their effects?

Additional possibilities for arts work

There are many rich opportunities for further cross arts work in this project. These include:

- Making masks of Blodin;
- Making a large puppet of Blodin, in the style of a Chinese dragon;[4]
- Creating a frieze in the style of the illustrator;
- Representing different aspects of Blodin through music – Blodin stalking the land; Blodin breathing fire and destroying villages; Blodin asleep and awakening; Blodin being destroyed by the river.

The project as outlined lends itself very well to performance as the raw material has largely been created. Children can share in the structuring, direction and choreography of the performance by suggesting a sequence to the activities and by suggesting/writing or selecting from the story any additional connecting passages they think might be needed.

Figure 6.3 The beast approaches

Creativity and the arts: allies in the curriculum?

The report *All Our Futures: Creativity, Culture and Education* was published in the UK in 1999.[5] The definition it offered of creativity – imaginative activity fashioned so as to produce outcomes that are original and of value – has since become widely accepted in educational circles. Official response was initially muted but the report was immediately welcomed in the UK by professional bodies. The fact that the National Union of Teachers commissioned a summarised version of its 200 pages to distribute to its members was an early indication of the groundswell of interest it generated, emanating from the teaching profession rather than from government directives. The reason behind this sudden professional interest in creativity is illuminated by Anna Craft, whose own book was published in 2000.[6] In 1991, a survey into teachers' attitudes towards creativity had demonstrated that only 17 per cent expressed any positive interest in it (Craft 2000: 112). The notable change evident by the end of the decade is documented by Craft as being largely due to the pressures felt by teachers from above, as typified by experiences of Ofsted. An agenda relating to creativity, she suggests, offered teachers the opportunity to reclaim 'lost parts of their professional life' (2000: 106), a chance to rediscover a sense of their own professional artistry and personal values.

The official guidance on creativity that has been provided since 2000,[7] while acknowledging the personal and social benefits of creativity, finds its ideological foundation in the needs of business and the economy. For example, under the heading, 'Creativity: Why Promote It?' the Qualifications and Curriculum Authority (QCA) offers the following commentary.

> Creativity can also promote economic development through promoting an entrepreneurial culture. Governments around the world have recognized that creativity is essential to economic competitiveness and a high value is placed on intellectual capital. Curricula and teaching methods are being developed to meet this goal. (2003: 2)

It goes on to stress how pupils need to be given the opportunity to become 'creative, innovative, enterprising' (p. 2). So the current consensus that favours creativity actually embraces competing educational values but the result is that everyone – business leaders, government ministers and teachers – can agree that creativity is a good thing. What is also agreed is that it should be of concern to all teachers and is no longer the prerogative of those subjects such as the arts that have traditionally viewed themselves as 'creative'. The clear message is that any subject discipline can be taught creatively, and that creativity can be taught through any subject discipline. Paradoxically, therefore, the recent emergence of creativity in educational discourse, rather than being seen as helpful for the position of the arts in the curriculum, could possibly act to further marginalise its status. By stressing how creative values should be part of every subject, the implication is plain that the arts are not necessary in order to promote them.

This may seem reasonable enough. To suggest that scientists, industrialists and historians are incapable of creativity as defined in *All Our Futures* is clearly absurd, as well as smacking of the kind of binary oppositional thinking criticised in the previous chapter. However, it is possible to raise real objections to any conscious attempt to relegate the arts from holding a central position in an education for creativity. For one thing, such a relegation is to deny the reality of western cultural history over the past five centuries, for the historical meanings surrounding the evolution of the concept of creativity were very specifically embedded within the arts. As Raymond Williams informs us, until the Renaissance, the verb 'to create' was limited to the idea of God's creation itself.[8] In the sixteenth century, however, the verb began to be applied to creations of the human imagination, in particular, the work of poets. The idea took hold that, in making humankind in his image, God had endowed it with his own urge to create. The term *creative* itself was not coined until the eighteenth century, Williams tells us, and again it was specifically related to the arts. 'High is our calling, friend, Creative Art' as Wordsworth felt able to write to his friend, the painter, Haydon (Williams 1976: 83). This close alliance between the arts, the imagination and being creative persisted well into the twentieth century when the term *creativity* first came into usage and writers such as Drucker began to apply it to other fields, notably business and management theory.

Given this history of the term, it is hardly surprising that an assumed association between the arts and creativity should be culturally persistent. Indeed, what we are faced with in a definition of creativity that actively disassociates itself from the arts is, in effect, a *re*definition that has decontextualised certain aspects such as innovation and imagination from the arts in order to apply them to a broader range of human activity. It is not without reason, therefore, that many teachers who have a particular interest in the arts feel that there is little to distinguish what they have long understood simply as good practice from what is now being touted as 'creative teaching'. The production and appreciation of original works of the imagination have understandably not been seen as priorities in the maths or history classroom, whereas they have always been seen as desired outcomes in the drama, art or poetry class. This is because, for reasons of culture and tradition, such outcomes have long been of central concern to them. As a result, conscientious teachers of the arts are used to grappling with questions related to teaching children ways of giving shape to their imaginative ideas and what it might mean to be original within the structures of their disciplines. The application of creativity to the history classroom, on the other hand, necessitates a re-contextualisation of principles deemed 'creative' through a process that is of necessity more convoluted. Take these examples drawn from the QCA guidance on teaching strategies to promote pupils' creativity in history.

- helping pupils make connections with their personal experiences;
- changing direction to inject new energy or ideas into pupils' work;
- helping pupils to find their own problems or challenges by suggesting 'what if . . .?';
- making clear to pupils that there is no right or wrong answer. (2003: 12)

Such strategies are long established in drama teaching. This is not to say that subjects such as history will not benefit from them, simply to reaffirm that, for cultural reasons, they are already part and parcel of an existing tradition of good teaching in the arts (which, of course, is not to deny the reality of bad teaching in the arts).

The theories of Howard Gardner can also be used to argue that the arts – and in particular drama – are of central value in the development of children's creativity.[9] The significance of his theory of multiple intelligences is recognized in *All Our Futures* and in the work of Anna Craft. He suggests that there are at least seven distinct forms of intelligence: linguistic, mathematical, spatial, kinaesthetic, musical, interpersonal and intrapersonal. So a child with a highly developed kinaesthetic intelligence learns best physically, through movement. If she also displays interpersonal intelligence, she will be very good at reading people's emotions and understanding human relationships. The fact that education has traditionally assessed intelligence in terms of linguistic and mathematical capability is, then, both erroneous and harmful to those children whose intellectual aptitudes lie in other areas. The theory provides strong support for drama as a learning medium. Because its forms of expression are multifaceted, involving language, movement, space, sound, individual and group work, drama opens up different pathways for children with different intellectual aptitudes to find ways of engaging imaginatively with its content. For the same reason, it offers children forms of expression other than the linguistic to give shape to their creative thinking. So the two very different fields of cultural history and psychology present us with strong arguments for positioning drama at the heart of a curriculum for creativity.

Drama, culture and creativity

Recent research has argued that human creativity is biologically located in the right hemisphere of the brain (see Craft 2000: 14–16). Whatever the reality of its biology, however, humans, unlike God, cannot create in a vacuum; they can only be creative from within cultural frameworks. If I decide to write a love song, for example, there is a range of musical traditions, from opera to soul, that could influence how I write it. Even if I produce a song that is judged to be ground-breakingly good, I will have used these traditions as my springboard to create something deemed to be original and of value. The fact that culture is central in affording anyone the possibility to be creative is true in science and technology as well as the arts, as all these disciplines exist within histories of experimentation and recognized achievement. It is for this reason that *All Our Futures* places equal emphasis on both culture and creativity, although the interest it inspired has tended to focus upon the latter at the expense of the former.

The problem for teachers here lies in the plurality of cultures that characterise classrooms in our increasingly globalised communities. Cultures are not mono-lithic entities whose forms we can present as solid, fixed and true; on the con-trary, different cultural traditions are merging, fusing and giving rise to new and varied forms of expression. This fact is emphasised in *All Our Futures*, which describes our social culture as 'dynamic, diverse and . . . evolving' (p. 42). If we accept Gardner's theories, then children's creative potential is intricately bound to their differing intellectual aptitudes. Similarly, the ways in which they will express their creativity will be strongly influenced by their cultural background and experiences. The challenge, then, for teachers who wish to use drama to develop children's creativity is twofold: to ensure that the forms presented are varied enough to offer different types of expression, in movement, language, sound and spatial design; and loose enough to allow children to bring their own cultural understandings of movement, music and language into play when using them.

Developing creativity through drama

If there is of necessity a complex, mutual relationship between creativity and culture, the same must also be true of the relationship between concept and form. There is no clear distinction between the process of creative thinking and cre-ative doing in drama; playing and trying to give expressive form to ideas is thought-in-action, characteristic of the kind of struggle that best defines the cre-ative process. It is this concept of struggle between mutually dependent qualities that I wish to use in order to analyse how elements of the *Blodin* project can be understood as education for creativity. This type of analysis is, I think, important in order to avoid the temptation of applying the definition of creativity too broadly to our teaching. To conflate good practice with creative practice, a ten-dency prevalent in the literature of creativity, serves to obfuscate rather than illu-minate what teaching for creativity actually consists of.

Convention and innovation

Craft sees 'possibility thinking' as being at the heart of creativity, and this kind of thinking as driven by the imagination. *All Our Futures* defines imaginative activity as 'the process of generating something original: providing an alternative to the expected, the conventional or the routine' (p. 29), and Craft, too, stresses the quality of going beyond the obvious, of breaking convention. She suggests two implications for classroom practice to foster the imagination:

> teachers stimulating and encouraging non-conventionality, whilst also encouraging children to understand the nature of conventions so that when they are being original in their own or wider terms, they can identify this. (2000: 5)

The relationship between convention and originality is surely subtler than these quotes suggest. Our society, driven by the values of mass consumption, prizes novelty very highly. Consequently, being described as 'conventional' has negative overtones, of being boring and predictable. But conventions are a necessary part of any cultural form, including drama, just as words and grammar are a necessary part of language. They are enabling as they provide the structures through which we can communicate meaning. It would be nonsensical to describe a poem that made use of a freeflow stream of consciousness as more creative than one of Keats's sonnets simply because it was less conventional. It is precisely in a struggle with convention that an artist's creativity is likely to gain expression. In other words, children cannot be creative in drama or poetry or any art form by being asked to express themselves without being introduced to forms through which they can do so. They must have some mastery of conventions before they can meaningfully be expected to use them innovatively.

Blodin provides a number of examples of children being asked to work at various points along the line between the conventional and the innovative. In (1d) they are introduced to the conventions of physical chorus work; in (4b) to vocal choric work. In each case the convention is at first modelled so that children can understand its possibilities. They are then given a focused task in which to play with some possibilities before shaping their performance. If a group produces something interesting that is also in some way different from the work of other groups, this can be signalled to the class, who can be asked to comment on *how* it is different and how this makes it effective. Children are deliberately challenged to produce something different in the warm-up activities in (2b) and (3d). Here in being challenged to respond physically to different words, such as *mountain, eagle, cliff*, etc, they are being helped to move from mimetic into abstract movement. This can be a strong imaginative leap for many children and is a good example of how an artistic convention can enable creativity by offering children expressive choices they were previously unaware of.

From play into form

While being careful not to conflate creativity with play, Craft explores in some detail the relationship between the two. She suggests that they both share an 'openness to possibilities' (p. 52), with social play and play that demands non-standardised responses being most conducive to creativity. In being asked to bring form to an idea, children will often need time to play with possibilities. This is particularly true when they are being introduced to new forms of expression. In (1c) and (4c) children are introduced to working with cloth and flags and will need time and encouragement to play with and share the possible visual effects they can offer before they can be expected to be creative with them. This approach complies with Hutt's notion, backed by Duffy (1998: 78) of *epistemic* and *ludic* play.[10] In epistemic play children investigate possibilities in new materials and engage in ludic play when they know what the material can do and practise making use of it.

A useful way of enabling children to shape their play creatively into form is to provide focus by limiting their choices. This is a principle very evident in poetry, where different poetic conventions make different formal demands of the poet. The challenges that boundary the play in (2b) and (3d) – that each child must be on a different level; or that the movement must include a change of pace, for example – are challenges that give direction to it. As children over time become more informed and able to manipulate these aspects of form, the teacher can introduce more complex challenges. Interestingly, play of this kind is illustrative of the two types of play that Craft sees as particularly conducive to creativity. It is social in its nature and the required responses, though clearly focused, are not at all 'standardised'.

Teachers' creativity and children's creativity

The current drive on creativity is as much directed towards teachers as it is towards children. As expressed in *All Our Futures*, 'Teaching for creativity involves teaching creatively' (p. 90). But my own creativity as a teacher need not always be aimed at developing creativity in the children. I will legitimately have other aims and creativity need not always be at the top of my agenda. The fact that the story is read to the children to the accompaniment of an appropriate musical soundtrack might be seen as creative on the teacher's part, but it is intended to enhance the children's engagement with the story, not to develop their creativity. Activity (3d) is a good example of teacher and pupil creativity working in tandem, or, as Duffy puts it, of the teacher 'intervening with sensitivity' (1998: 94) The mapping activity and the teacher's questioning is intended to draw out language from the children, to help them create phrases they would not readily think of. When the movement motifs are complete, children take joint responsibility for shaping the finished choreographed piece, with the teacher acting in an advisory capacity. If at the end of the project you decide to fashion the work into a performance, this principle of joint creative endeavour is a good one to follow.

Security and risk-taking

Literature on creativity emphasises how risk taking is an integral part of the creative process and how an environment of trust is therefore necessary for children to feel secure enough to 'dare to be different'. The onus here is on the teacher to create this environment, and it is especially important if children are being asked to perform to their peers. The form of feedback described in (1d) is intended to foster such trust. Children must learn to give praise and to receive it; they do not choose whom they praise or who praises them; and critical feedback remains positive at all times.

If, as *All Our Futures* suggests, creative outcomes must be 'of value', then critical evaluation must be an integral part of the creative process. This feedback framework described here fosters children's evaluative skills in a positive way, encouraging them to look for and explain what they like in others' work. Once an environment of trust has been established, the teacher can begin to challenge the class, to make it clear that she expects children to surprise her, to dare to be different. But this does not imply loosening the focus of an activity. Research has shown that children need to have a clear understanding both of the purposes of an activity and of the teacher's expectations if they are to respond creatively to its challenges (see Craft 2000: 113).

The individual and the group

Individual creativity is affected by dialogue with others. By working in pairs or in groups, children are constantly negotiating how to respond to a particular challenge. When watching other groups, they can be encouraged to learn from the things they praise and to feel free to copy any good ideas. In more complex group work, it is helpful, therefore, to allow children to watch each other's work in draft form, as work in progress. In, for example, (3d) one group might enjoy the way another group has concentrated on movement whereas they have begun by developing the vocal work. The two groups are then able to learn from one another and have the opportunity to develop these aspects of their own work.

Providing time and setting deadlines

The fact that creative ideas take time to generate is emphasised by Craft and echoed in *All Our Futures*. The fact remains, however, that tight deadlines can concentrate the mind in ways that can stimulate creative responses. In all of the activities in this project, the pace should be brisk but the project as a whole will benefit from the kind of flexible school timetabling recommended by Ofsted (2003). Such flexibility will allow for activities to take place in a logical order and for ideas in one activity to stimulate creativity in another. A good example of this is how the landscape poetry (3e) can flow directly out of the movement and vocal work (in 3d) and will be both more vibrant and completed more quickly.

Convergent and divergent thinking

In discussing research into the two hemispheres of the brain, Craft usefully summarises the current wisdom; that the left hemisphere is chiefly responsible for controlling the more verbal, logical, analytical aspects of human action whereas the right hemisphere controls the more artistic, emotional, non-verbal aspects. These can be loosely related to the contrast between *convergent* thinking, or thinking directed towards finding possibilities that fit a set of needs, and *divergent* thinking, concerned with alternatives, possibilities and intuition (p. 32). Craft is, however, right to challenge the over-simplistic tendency to label divergent thinking as creative and convergent thinking as non-creative. It is demonstrable that both types of thinking contribute to creative outcomes. In (1e) for example, the teacher's questioning encourages children to think divergently – to imagine what Shanga might be weaving – and convergently – to follow through the logical implications as to what their suggestions imply. A more typical example is in (2c). Here the children are experimenting with the possibilities that sound recorder offers them while, at the same time, selecting those which fit a prescribed outcome, namely, the voice of Blodin. This interrelationship of convergent and divergent thinking, of logical and intuitive thought, seems to be characteristic of the kind of purposeful play that typifies the performance related activities at the heart of this project.

Conclusion

The argument throughout this section has been that, despite the drive to encourage creativity across the curriculum, the arts, and more specifically drama, ought to be seen as a major means for encouraging children to think and express themselves creatively. I am acutely aware of areas I have not discussed, in particular the complex area of aesthetics and its relationship to creativity in the arts. It is important that such a study should continue and that the arts should not be side-lined in the fashionable dash to creativity that characterises the current educational mood. Through the broad area of the arts, I would argue, not only can children learn to be creative but in being creative they can also locate themselves at a critical distance from an entrepreneurial culture that often seems to value their creative potential for economic and utilitarian reasons alone. The question: 'Creativity – for what purpose?' is one that teachers should continue to ask.

Notes

1 M. Morpurgo, *Blodin the Beast*, London, Frances Lincoln, 1995.

2 See also the section on Assessment in Chapter 7.

3 In C. Buckton and P. Corbett, *Focus English: Anthology 5*, Oxford, Heinemann, 1998. Originally published in K. Wright, *Cat Among the Pigeons*, London, Viking Press, 1987.

4 See C. Astell-Burt, *I am the Story*, London, Souvenir Press, 2002.

5 The Report of the National Advisory Committee on Creative and Cultural Education, DfEE Publications.

6 A. Craft, *Creativity Across the Primary Curriculum*, London, RoutledgeFalmer, 2000.

7 Qualifications and Curriculum Authority, *Creativity Across the Curriculum* 2003; Ofsted, *Expecting the Unexpected*, 2003.

8 R. Williams, *Keywords*, London, Fontana Paperbacks, 1976.

9 H. Gardner, *Frames of Mind: The Theory of Multiple Intelligences*, London, Fontana, 1993.

10 B. Duffy, *Supporting Creativity and Imagination in the Early Years*, Buckingham, Open University Press, 1998.

Evaluation in context

Assessing the projects

The projects are designed to be flexible enough for adaptation across a number of year groups. However, the learning objectives presented in the text for each are specific to the year group and, with regard to the National Literacy Strategy, the term in which they were originally taught. These can easily be modified. For example, if the project in Chapter 3 were to be taught to a Year 3 rather than a Year 1 class, then a quick glance at NLS guidance for Year 3, Term 3 will show the following teaching objectives as immediately relevant: T1, T2; T3; T4; T5; T10; T11; T12; T13.

There are, of course, a number of sources from which teachers within England and Wales are currently asked to draw their objectives. For English there is the National Curriculum, the National Literacy Strategy and the recently published objectives for Speaking and Listening.[1] For drama the guidance is even more diverse, including all of the above but also guidance issued by the QCA[2] and the recently revised publication *Drama in Schools*.[3] The problem here is that the objectives do not always readily complement one another. The statutory guidance for speaking and listening contained within the National Curriculum, for example, readily lends itself to the kind of holistic, integrated planning that these topics embody, also encouraged in the current drive towards creative approaches to teaching and learning. The recent objectives from the DfES, however, present a very different model for teaching speaking and listening, recommending one specific objective per term for each of the complementary areas of speaking, listening, group discussion and interaction, and drama. This more rigid model fits less easily within an integrated approach to curriculum planning.

The only sensible response to this surfeit of objectives is to be flexible in one's use of them and to remember that there is a lot more to good teaching than matching up teaching content alongside a string of letters and numbers. Below is the format for assessment devised by Pat, the teacher of the Year 5 children with whom I taught the *Blodin* project outlined in Chapter 6.

Assessment

1. Day to day (formative) assessment of learning objectives during scaffolding activities
2. Summative assessment of learning objectives linked to extended writing

Numbers refer to National Literacy Strategy except Speaking and Listening (written below) where they refer to the recently published recommended guidance.

48 Speaking
to tell a story using notes designed to cue techniques, such as repetition, recap and humour

51 Drama
to perform a scripted scene making use of dramatic conventions

54 Drama
to reflect on how working in role helps to explore complex issues

55 Speaking
to present a spoken argument, sequencing points logically, defending views with evidence and making use of persuasive language

57 Drama
to use and recognise the impact of theatrical effects in drama

The Genre sheet below was devised with the class to provide guidance for their Formative Assessment in the narrative strand. Similar sheets were devised for poetry, playscript and persuasive writing.

TEXT TYPE

NARRATIVE

PURPOSE

ENTERTAIN

AUDIENCE

CHILDREN IN PARALLEL CLASS

STRUCTURE

PLOT – Exposition
– Complication
– Climax
– Resolution
Chronological (except Timeslip stories)

PARAGRAPHS

TITLE

LANGUAGE FEATURES

Past Tense
First person or third person
Description of characters and setting (using powerful
Adjectives, Adverbs, Similes)
Some Dialogue (speech marks)
Connectives in compound sentences

SHARED	SCAFFOLDED (Supported composition and modelling)	EXTENDED	LITERACY TEXT OBJECTIVES
Drama and Blodin story	Plot line Character chants	NARRATIVE Own story based on Blodin	Term 1 – Reading 1, 2, 3, 9, 10, 11 – Writing 13, 14, 15 – Speaking and Listening 48 (Speaking) Term 2 – Reading 2, 3 – Writing 7, 8, 9, 10 Term 3 – Speaking and Listening 57 (Drama)
	Landscape Poem In my carpet I will weave … Chants	POETRY Narrative – Blodin Tale	Term 1 – Reading 8, 9, 10 – Writing 13, 14, 16, 17 Term 2 – Reading 2, 4
	Villagers/Shanga	PLAYSCRIPT Assembly version	Term 1 – Reading 5, 9, 10 – Writing 13, 14, 18, 19, 20 – Speaking and Listening 51 (Drama) Term 2 – Reading 2
	Hardgit's letter Poster-friends of Blodin	PERSUASIVE WRITING School/Town environment Class debate (Citizenship) Leaflet about recycling	Term 1 – Reading 9, 10 – Writing 13, 14 Term 2 – Reading 2 – Speaking and Listening 54 (Drama) Term 3 – Reading 15 – Writing 17, 19 – Speaking and Listening 55 (Speaking)

Figure 7.1

This model of assessment has a number of features to recommend it. First and foremost, it demonstrates a flexible approach to using national guidance on objectives in order to inform the teaching content, abandoning any unnecessarily rigid adherence to the termly plans for both the *NLS* and the *Speaking, Listening, Learning* objectives. This flexibility is, however, matched by a rigour in planning, assessing and recording children's achievement. The reading, writing, speaking and listening activities are carefully and concisely matched to specific objectives in ways which illustrate and facilitate the integration of the drama and English work. The genre sheet on narrative demonstrates how assessment can be both formative and summative and, more importantly, how such frameworks, when shared with children, can guide their understanding as to what specific skills they are being asked to demonstrate in a particular task. The nature of these projects and the kind of assessment they encourage, across a range of speaking, listening and writing frames, makes them highly suitable as introductory or revision topics as they relate to a skills-based curriculum. Their content, I would argue, and the deeper issues they approach, make them suitable for any time of the academic year.

Evaluating the projects

Although outcomes-based assessment is fundamental to successful teaching and learning, it is far from the whole picture. There are many fundamental educational aims that we associate with children's personal development: their growth in self-confidence, in social awareness, in creativity, for example. All of these have been seen as intrinsic to the broad aims of these projects, yet none of them are we comfortably able to assess, or test, by reducing them to simple, clear, incremental objectives. How we note progress in these qualities as teachers will vary, but in one way or another it is likely to take some kind of narrative form, based upon observations made in particular contexts, referring back to previously observed behaviour and forward to help shape future actions.

When we evaluate a scheme of work, we do something closely related to this but qualitatively different. First of all, we concentrate on our own performance as teachers, asking ourselves how good a scheme it was, where it was particularly strong and where we might make improvements. Issues of objectives-led assessment will of course be relevant to how we judge the value of a scheme but the more elusive outcomes of teaching, those beyond the assessment of pre-planned objectives, may well be what strike us most powerfully. And these evaluations may be centred upon individuals, upon a specific group of pupils or upon the class as a whole. Such evaluations are highly significant to teachers because they inform future pedagogy; if I find that something has worked well, I will want to try it again some time. More than this, I will be interested in understanding *why* it has worked so that I can apply my new understanding to other projects, other schemes of work.

These projects were judged as highly successful by both myself and the class teachers involved, and part of our subsequent evaluations led to their current, revised formats. On a deeper level, however, how specific children or groups of children responded to the work led us to talk, speculate, enthuse, puzzle and wonder. Such is the stuff of professional evaluation. It is central to what makes us professionals, to what we believe to be of value in what we do. I have therefore chosen to conclude the book by looking at three issues of professional interest that emerged from these evaluations. In addressing two of the issues, I have concentrated on the observations and informed conclusions of the two class teachers involved. The first of these centres around one child, David, identified as having specific learning difficulties, whereas the second concentrates upon the performance of the boys as a group throughout the project. The third issue relates to the complex area of cultural identity and how it can impinge upon children's drama work. In addressing this final issue, I spent more time researching and interrogating the evidence myself, taking advantage of the opportunity my post in a university affords me, to investigate and probe complex issues of cultural and educational significance and to share my conclusions with others.

Issue 1: David, a boy with learning difficulties

David was a six-year-old boy in the class where we developed the project on 'The Selfish Giant'. He had been assessed as having two conditions that impeded his learning, one linguistic the other social. The first was a speech and communication problem, specifically related to the ordering of language and sound. His speech was unclear and, as Debbie, his class teacher, put it, the filing system for vocabulary in his brain was disorganised, which led him to file words in the wrong place and consequently have difficulties in retrieving them. His verbal comprehension (including receptive language and his understanding of oral instructions involving basic language concepts) had been assessed at 3 years 10 months, whereas his naming vocabulary, which included expressive vocabulary, was 3 years 1 month. His writing was below Level 1.

David had great difficulties in relating to and interacting with his peer group. He would talk confidently in school to adults such as myself and his teacher because, as Debbie explained, we would listen to him and show interest in what he had to say. This was not true of his peer group. Because of his difficulties in communicating, he found it difficult to listen and liked to push his own agenda in group work or ordinary conversation. Learning to wait and take turns was one of his specified targets.

He idolised his grandfather, who had fought in World War II. War was a particular obsession of his, as were anything to do with *Star Wars*, dinosaurs and devils. As the rest of the class did not share in these interests, he would often retreat into himself, into what his teacher saw as an obsessive fantasy world.

David was noted as having a 'very vivid imagination', although Debbie did worry about the narrow focus of interest it tended to centre around. If he did find a point of interest, he could develop his own agenda quickly, usually bending it into these fantasy obsessions.

He was also identified as having very good spatial and non-verbal reasoning skills, assessed at over 8 years, and Debbie commented upon his impressive ability for memorising and reproducing pictures.

His IEP (individual education profile) had identified the following targets for his teacher:

- To help him develop listener/other awareness;
- To provide him with activities to develop his listening/short-term memory skills;
- To use visual prompts to assist his comprehension when possible.

Below is an extract from the journal I kept throughout this project, commenting on David's work in Activities (4:4g, i).

> David worked quite well in music, choosing a big drum and getting the hang of the rhythm well, which is interesting given the fact that his group work is weak. Perhaps this was because both the listening and the interaction with others was non-verbal in nature. Perhaps, too, the 'spatial' quality of rhythm helped him access its demands. He was in the second group in the garden centre, before that he spent some time drawing pictures of war, parachutes, etc. – his second such picture of the day! He lives in a house with his father and older brother – no women. Debbie tells me he can name every dinosaur but not all of the children in his class. He quickly gets obsessive. In the garden centre, for example, he questioned me continuously about the presence of my tape recorder and what I was using it for. Eventually he joined in the role play but really did need my direction and support to help him work with the others. He was very willing to write in role about what his job in the garden would be and when he would carry it out. His job, he informed me, was to make sure that the plants got the right amount of sun. I asked him to read what he had written to me and it did demonstrate an understanding of his science work. He spoke willingly to me throughout, with evidence of what Debbie has indicated as his struggle to find the correct word, especially whenever he felt in competition with other children to get his thoughts out.

In discussing the value of the drama for David at the end of the project with me, Debbie reached the following conclusions:

- David has great difficulty remembering a story in printed form, even if it is read to him. His keen visual and spatial awareness, however, had enabled him to concentrate and recall the events of the story when presented in dramatic form. The same was true of the storytelling moments (4:3a; 4b; 5a). The visual and spatial elements of this kind of storytelling had kept him focused and listening.

- Although David has problems listening to his peers, the fact that he will listen to the teacher meant that the teacher's role for him was crucial in the drama. My use of teacher in role had been a powerful learning tool in his case, gripping his attention and helping to focus his considerable imaginative powers.

- David enjoyed the strongly dramatic aspects – the scowling giant and the fierceness of his anger in (4:1e). Such moments had been key in keeping his imagination focused away from his usual images of violent fantasy, providing him with what Debbie judged to be a richer imaginative experience for the duration of the drama.

- David enjoys being the centre of attention and the whole class drama work had been a platform for him to volunteer his own thoughts and be physically very active. He had been the first to volunteer an answer as to why the Giant had put the sign up (4:1c), because the children might have left crisp packets and bottles around; he had shown a strong appreciation of how the volunteers should stand as railings, telling them to be thinner and more straight (4:2a). Other children in the class were not as forthcoming and they were often content to let him take the lead. Although this provided space for him to be seen and heard, it did not, however, address the other of his fundamental needs, that of learning socially to interact with his peers.

- In group work he had continued to have difficulty in listening to and working with his peers, tending to keep to his own agenda. For example, he insisted on being a guard tower (his idea) although the rest of the group were trying to form a prickly hedge! (4:2a)

- All children were asked to complete an extended written task (related to national assessment demands) soon after the project. Its theme – a story in which someone's character changes – was evidently related to but could not be a retelling of the story of 'The Selfish Giant'. There was no evident improvement in the overall quality of his writing here, although he did write substantially more than was usual for him. However, in the smaller, less formal writing tasks that he had been asked to do during the project (such as in the garden centre, described above) he did show a sense of focus, a willingness to write and to attempt new words and an understanding of the purpose of the writing.

In conclusion, Debbie felt that David had benefited greatly from the project. Although there had been no dramatic improvement in his written and social skills, it had provided opportunities for him to learn from his strengths, through spatial and visual awareness and strong imaginative engagement. Drama allowed some of his specific IEP targets, in the areas of language and social development, to be addressed directly within a context where he could feel he was succeeding much of the time. Although recognizing that drama could never address the full range of his learning difficulties, she believed there would be a payoff over time from regular drama work, in the direction she had already seen demonstrated by many of the children.

> They've remembered words like 'scowling' and 'fierce' because they've seen and experienced them. They've seen how the giant was feeling, they've heard him shouting and they know why he was feeling that way. So they've understood the meaning of the words. They've remembered them and they've used them in their speaking and in their writing.

Issue 2: The boys of 5P

In setting up the drama project 'The Forbidden Planet' (5:1a) Femi, the class teacher, was horrified. She began with a blank canvas, telling the children they could choose the jobs they would like on the space ship. When I received the applications, she was most apologetic. All the girls had applied to be cooks, waitresses and nurses. Boys, on the other hand, wanted to be guards, pilots and scientists. All the problems of restrictive gender roles, so eloquently argued by Sharon Grady,[4] were evident and we hadn't even begun! Fortunately I was able to tell her that in this drama these roles were chiefly a means of engaging the children with the story and that issues of power and gender would be examined as they related to the characters they would later meet. But Femi, a British South Asian woman herself, felt she had learned an important lesson for her future teaching.

Judging when and how to challenge limiting gender expectations is far from simple and needs to be done sensitively, over time and within the parameters of a whole school policy if it is to have any lasting effect. Pat, the class teacher with whom I taught the *Blodin* project, also saw gender as a key issue in her evaluation of the project but in a different sense. Her school had a documented problem of boys' underachievement. At the age of 7, between 60 and 70 per cent of the boys were consistently failing to reach the target Level 2 in literacy. What she had seen in this project, however, was 'quite extraordinary levels of engagement' from the girls *and* the boys. This had spilled over into their writing and into the assembly that the children had prepared on the story during the week after the project, where overall written and spoken language performance was far higher than she had anticipated. But it was the response of the boys that particularly intrigued her and it was here that she wished to focus the post-project evaluation. She drew a series of conclusions, listed and examined below, supported by material drawn from an interview I conducted with a group of boys and referenced by the recent Ofsted publication *Yes He Can! Schools Where Boys Write Well*,[5] which the school was consulting to help tackle this particular issue.

The story itself had appeal

The boys I interviewed spoke enthusiastically of the story's excitement, its mystery and also the moments of suspense in the story itself and within the drama. Ofsted, too, refer to the need for teachers to value fast-paced stories of adventure and the macabre, the kind that boys generally appear to enjoy (para. 31).

The drama provided a physical and active approach to learning

In Pat's words:

> Drama was like a hook to hang the vocabulary onto. When using it later, they would often refer back to the physical work they did and to the exercises where they had used repetition a lot, expanding and broadening their vocabulary and also testing it out.

She felt that this physicality was 'a vehicle, a way forward' for all of the children but particularly so for the boys. She believed that girls were used to verbalising in their play but that boys tended to be less so.[6] Particularly significant she thought was how language and physicality fused in the drama work. As she said, 'the whole environment was visual, kinaesthetic and verbal'. This physical aspect of the work was indeed particularly enjoyed by the boys. Their reasons for this included the fact that they were being challenged to be in control of their bodies, that they were being asked 'to think different from usual' and that they were spending time away from their desks!

The language tasks were clearly delineated and concise in nature

Ofsted note that writing tasks should vary in their demands and that succinctness as much as elaboration and description should be valued. They write:

Boys often complain that teachers are only interested in the length of their writing and dismiss short answers out of hand. (para. 32)

When I asked the boys if they felt that the physical work helped their writing, there was a pause before one of them made a humorous but telling comment in line with Ofsted findings.

> In some ways, when you play with the words, it helps. And when you shorten the sentences [see 6:4c] it makes such a change from, say, being told to turn 'the cat sat on the mat' into erm 'the furry white cat sat on the explosive mat'.

Writing tasks had real purpose and were firmly embedded in context

Here Pat referred specifically to the scripting (6:1f) and the letter (6:3b) where she felt the writing was 'absolutely in context, with everyone understanding the reason for doing it'. There were two associated issues here she thought: the value of striking a balance between presenting models and offering choices; and the value of teaching the project as an integrated block. The letter writing, she felt, had presented the class with latitude and allowed individual boys to write from a genuinely held stance, not simply from a perspective dictated by the teacher or under pressure from their peers. In this way, their opinions weren't 'stamped down' before even finding expression. Ofsted (para. 42) note how boys generally enjoy being offered choice as to content and expression but respond well to a request to keep within stated formal and structural constraints.

The fact that the work was organized as a block meant that tasks occurred in a logical sequence. Ofsted make specific reference to the importance for teachers to make skilful links between reading and writing tasks (para. 41); and to use oral work as a prelude to writing, with a conscious attempt to teach vocabulary (para. 41). The framework for this project did all of this, Pat felt, and more as it also created and sustained a meaningful context throughout its development. As a result, writing occurred not simply because it was now a lesson where we write but because it made sense to the children to write at this particular point in the scheme.

The overall ethos was one of high expectations but also protection from failure

'Expectations were high throughout', said Pat. 'Simple words like "scared" were never accepted as enough. The children were asked to offer something different. "Surprise me!" you'd say.' Having high but achievable expectations was appreciated by the boys particularly within the context of the physical work. 'Everybody does the same shape and you make us delete that and try something else. You make us do something better, you tell us straight.' Pat felt that such challenging comments from the teacher worked because they were directed at the whole class, not at individuals, and never voiced negatively, as criticism. Children were also protected from peer group criticism throughout and Pat thought that this combination of high expectation and support was crucial in raising the boys' self-esteem. 'I wonder to what extent they have learned failure? The teacher has said "deliver this to me" and they can't?' The combination of support – in terms of planning, writing frames and collaborative opportunities – and challenge, also evident in writing tasks, is very much in line with Ofsted recommendations (para. 38).

I am, of course, aware of the potential drawbacks in addressing gender issues in a simple, binary manner. Aren't we in danger of essentialising the identities of boys, presuming them all to like the same kinds of stories, the same kind of physical activities? And what about challenging the stereotype rather than apparently accepting and working within it? Why not encourage them into broader gender roles, for their own good and that of society? In fairness, I think none of the conclusions drawn by Pat precludes any of this. In concerning herself with the reality of boys' underachievement in her class, she is not seeking pedagogical models that collude with misplaced machismo or that only seek to treat the boys as some kind of homogenous problem. A key factor discovered by Ofsted in schools where boys write well – one they describe as 'of immense importance' – was, in fact, a non-macho culture, where intellectual and aesthetic accomplishments were valued and expected from *all* children, whatever their gender (para. 9). And this is really the point. If we regard gender differences between girls and boys largely in terms of tendencies, fostered by culture and upbringing, in specifically addressing the perceived needs of one tendency, Pat is not denying the needs of the other. In recognizing the value of physicality in developing boys' vocabulary, for example, she believes girls can also benefit. If for cultural reasons boys on the whole tend to be linguistically less developed, they need more varied pedagogical models to extend their vocabulary. If these models work well for many of the boys, they can also work well for many of the girls. And by adopting more physical approaches, she does not intend to prioritise the boys' work over that of the girls. In this way, as well as boys (in general) being encouraged to improve in the area of language, she will be offering girls (in general) opportunities to be assertive within physical as well as conceptual space. Such an approach will help prevent what Grady has observed, the danger of girls being 'assigned to yet another inactive role in drama' (2000: 80).

Issue 3: Drama and multiple cultural competence

In the project 'The Forbidden Planet', the class teacher was enormously impressed, as I was, by the overall quality of the children's involvement in the drama and their ability to articulate its complex dilemmas. It is what I term these 'avenues of engagement' that I went on to analyse with reference to the cultural contexts of these children's lives as young British South Asians. In this task, I was fortunate to be able to draw upon the advice and expertise of my colleague Eleanor Nesbitt, an RE specialist in the University of Warwick and an internationally recognised expert on the cultural lives of British South Asian children. What I present below is an attempt to understand these children's engagement in the drama work as a process quite probably stimulated and enriched by their cultural identities.

I am fully aware that such an attempt is fraught with difficulties. For a start, where do we locate these cultural identities? Nesbitt (1998)[7] has pointed out that the identities of British-born and British-raised members of ethnic minorities are often theorised in a binary manner, described as falling 'between two cultures' or as 'bi-cultural'. She proposes the more complex concept of 'multiple cultural competence' and suggests that the identities of young British South Asians should be examined 'along at least the three axes of Britishness, Asianness and their religion' (p. 190). To follow even these categories is highly problematic in what must necessarily remain a brief and speculative analysis. Nevertheless, I believe that such an analysis, regarding 'multiple cultural competence' in a positive light, can help us understand how axes of cultural diversity might have helped these children engage with our version of Shakespeare's story. To assist me in my evaluation, I interviewed two groups of six children, one halfway through the project and the other at its conclusion. In the account that follows I will concentrate mainly, but not exclusively, on the responses, both inside and outside the drama, of three of the children I interviewed: Nasreen, a lively, confident and devout Muslim girl, who wore a veil at all times; Paramjeet, a Sikh boy, thoughtful and very articulate; and Sunil, a Hindu boy, very talkative and a confident, capable performer. All three were first-generation British-born with strong roots in the Punjab, where they visited close family relatives at least once a year.

The context of Punjabi culture

The drama was constructed to appeal to what I know, from practical experience, of eight- and nine-year-old children. It was rich in secrets, lies, magic, surprises, moments of comedy and moments of tension. This was intended to engage and hold the children's interest but could not ensure their comprehension of what remained a complex plot, despite my adaptations. One question to ask is whether their resource of stories might have contributed to the ability to grasp the issues that they so ably demonstrated.

All of the children interviewed told me that they watched a mixture of mainstream English language TV programmes for children, mainly cartoons, but that they also had access to Asian language programmes, including films, that their parents watched and that they watched occasionally. The plots of Bollywood films are often drawn from the rich tradition of Punjabi love stories that are also reflected in a popular genre of Urdu poetry called the *ghazal*. In them, romantic love is seen as a threat to the social order 'in a social system in which a high premium is placed on female chastity and marriages are arranged to create or strengthen socio-economic links between households'.[8] Their themes of 'ill-fated romance and star-crossed love' are enormously popular across the religious and language communities of the Punjab and those pictures of iconic figures hanging inside British South Asian homes that are not religious are most likely drawn from these tales. A popular edition is written by Gurbakhsh Singh,[9] and in the second of his stories, *Laila Majnu: The Pearl of Night,* Laila, the daughter of a chief, falls in love with Quais, the son of a family with whom her own house has been feuding for generations. At the beginning of the story we are told that Laila's beauty 'could dazzle any eyes during the day, but it was kept concealed under a veil. . . . At nightfall, discarding the veil and the inhibitions it imposed, Laila went around her garden caressing buds, blooms and plants' (p. 46). She sings a song to herself of a 'heavenly fountain at which lovers drank deep in the light of the moon', sighing and wondering to herself 'Where could this fountain be?' (p. 47). Laila, in her youth, innocence and yearning for love, could be Juliet; in her closeness to nature she could be Ophelia. Treat the culturally specific detail of the veil as symbolic of her isolation from young men at the time of her burgeoning sexuality, forcing her to spend time dreaming on her own, and we have a possible Miranda, with Quais as a potential Ferdinand.

Of course, I am not stating that these children were necessarily acquainted with this tale, but it is typical of a genre, highly popular in their community, clearly reminiscent of elements of *The Tempest* and other tales of Shakespeare. It is this potential rapport between the Asian and religious strands of their cultural identities and our version of *The Tempest* that I now wish to examine, concentrating on those issues and dilemmas where the rapport appears to have been strongest.

Patriarchal authority, marriage and family honour

In response to my question 'Is Prospero right not to let Miranda see Ferdinand?' Nasreen's first answer was a clear 'No!' Later, however, with no prompting, she seemed to reflect upon it from a specifically Muslim perspective on the practice of arranged marriages.

I think that's good because why does she just want to fall in love with him? If she had went on earth she could have like saw someone else that was related to her instead of talking to some-one who wasn't related to her.

Although we never made use of them in our drama, her sentiment carries echoes of Prospero's lines to Miranda:

> To the most of men this is a Caliban,
> And they to him are angels. (I. ii)

Both objections are based upon Miranda's perceived naivety, her ignorance of men, with Nasreen's emanating from her own ethnic and religious context, where the tradition of marriages arranged with relatives remains very strong.[10] As the stories of *Immortal Lovers* illustrate, there has always been the potential for tension in such a practice between the will of the individual and the authority of the family. Shaw examines how disputes over love and marriage in British Pakistani homes owe more to these stresses inherent to the culture itself and not necessarily to the desire of young Pakistani women to adopt western, liberal values (cf. pp. 185–93). In *The Tempest*, of course, family authority is equivalent to patriarchal authority and this, too, is resonant of many Muslim homes in Britain.

> Girls who elope or marry 'outside' . . . are in effect denying their fathers the opportunity to fulfil their duty to marry their daughters respectfully, as virgins. If there is no other way of salvaging reputation, a father and brothers may sever all links with the girl, to avoid being reminded of the shame. (Shaw 2000: 186)

Issues of family honour are further heightened in *The Tempest* as Ferdinand is the son of Prospero's enemy. In the forum session (5:5d), Nasreen volunteered to take on the role of Prospero and began with a strong attempt to assert her patriarchal will. This time she found Prospero's antipathy to the union in a conviction that Ferdinand was *'exactly the same as his father (who) left us on the planet'*. But in response to the protest of Miranda (teacher-in-role) that 'no-one can see inside someone's heart' she capitulated. *'Your choice is to see him or not'* were her final words, delivered in an equally authoritative tone. *'I'll let you make the decision.'* In the subsequent exercise (5:5e) she chose to sculpt a happy ending for Miranda and Ferdinand, insisting that the two join hands.

From the perspective of a white, liberal westerner, it might be tempting to see Nasreen's journey as empowering, one that allowed her to shift her position from support for a system that reduces a young woman's choice of marital partner to prioritising that very right to choose. The concept of multiple cultural competence, however, offers a different, less confrontational explanation and one that is less culturally arrogant. Simply put, the drama enabled Nasreen to display alternative cultural perspectives by offering her the chance to adopt and play with a different identity and to dialogue from within it. The fact that she quickly chose to let the daughter decide for herself suggests a readiness rather than a reluctance to shift perspective when the discourse moved on to a liberal agenda. In other words, she already possessed the competence to switch between authoritarian and liberal discourses and the drama offered her a channel of articulation rather than emancipation.

Not all children supported the idea of a happy ending. Two girls chose to disrupt the consensus of contentment in the images being sculpted in (5:5e). One moulded the two subjects into an image of unhappy partnership *'because he's like his father'* – Ferdinand scolding Miranda, his finger pointing in her direction, with Miranda looking dejected and upset. The belief in family likeness passing from one generation to the next, expressed by Nasreen above in the voice of Prospero, was very strong throughout the class and Paramjeet's comment: *'if Ferdinand's father's bad, he might be bad as well, because of the family relationship'* had widespread support. The second girl took this image a stage further, to the great delight of many of the children, sculpting a furious Ferdinand slapping Miranda. Unhappy marriages and marital breakdown are common in the UK and not uncommon in British South Asian families. The two girls were from Hindu and Sikh backgrounds respectively. Although these religious communities do not arrange marriages with close relatives and are perhaps more 'relaxed' in their approach to young people choosing their own partners, there still persists a strong desire to avoid a bad reputation. This concern with family honour – *izzat* – is very strong in Punjabi culture, particularly if the honour of a sister or a daughter is seen to be at stake. This can lead to an insistence on the part of parents that their children marry their first partner, who will not necessarily be the right partner, and this can be a cause of unhappy marriages and possible incidents of domestic violence.[11]

Sunil, a child who did not live with his father, nonetheless responded to this final, violent image by offering an interpretation that stressed the bond of family loyalty between father and son. *'Ferdinand has just learned that his father is Prospero's enemy.'* This primacy of family loyalty was most clearly expressed in children's reaction to Prospero's decision to forgive Antonio. Nasreen could sympathise with Antonio's feelings as she had an elder sister who *'keeps on being bossy to me, saying "you go and wash the dishes while I play."'* Although none of the children agreed that Antonio's grudges justified his abandonment of Prospero on the planet, in (5:5b) they demonstrated a range of reactions to his admission of treachery. Many were able to empathise with his jealousy even though he expressed no remorse for what he had done. *'Prospero got all the attention and he didn't,'* as one girl said. In their writing (5:5h), however, all children felt that Prospero's decision to forgive Antonio was just, with most agreeing with a Hindu girl who expressed it particularly clearly. '*He forgave Antonio because he was his brother. I think this is just, because you should always forgive your brother or sister.*' Possibly the most widespread of South Asian festivals in Britain is the brother–sister festival commonly known as *Raksha Bandhan* (literally, 'tying the bond') or by its Punjabi name *Rakhrai.* It is celebrated at home by all Hindu families and by many Sikh families around the time of August. In it, the sister ties an ornamental thread around her brother's wrist and the brother presents his sister with a gift, promising to protect her at all times. It is hardly surprising, therefore, that these children saw the bond between siblings as so important and that this Hindu girl expressed the sentiment so strongly.

Caliban: brother or 'other'?

Caliban's first appearance – his wrists bound, the evident squalor in which he lived, his cries of anguish – made a lasting impression on the children and at first they were moved to pity him. All of their sketches (in 5:3c) showed him in a sympathetic light, with Prospero as the harsh master. Paramjeet was highly indignant, '*He shows Prospero the magic stones, right, but then Prospero takes all the power and is bossing everyone around*', thus expressing a symbolic understanding of Prospero as coloniser, focusing on his appropriation of the planet's resources. The aspect of oppression that the children clearly felt most strongly was the fact that Caliban was forced to speak a language other than his own. In the words of Sunil: '*It's his planet and everyone on that planet should learn his language.*' This was supported by Paramjeet. '*People who come to England, they learn English!*' and he used his own language (Punjabi) as Caliban's in (5:3d)

> PROSPERO: (angrily and nastily)
> Do all the jobs starting with these logs!
> CALIBAN: (bravely)
> Nei appey chuckie![12]

This appreciation of language as a site of resistance was expressed differently by Nasreen, who thought she understood why Prospero prevented Caliban from speaking his own. '*Caliban might have said something bad in his own language and Prospero might think it's bad*' – an authority's fear of being mocked or subverted in a language it cannot understand.

Issues of language can be complex in British South Asian families. When I asked children in the second interview which of their languages they felt to be more important, their responses – Urdu, Gujurati or English – depended upon which language was chiefly spoken at home. None hesitated, however, in giving the answer 'English' when asked which was the most important language at school. Parents born in South Asia see it as important to speak their native language at home whereas their bilingual children will sometimes refuse to, seeing English as the language of power and status.[13] What the children in the first interview particularly objected to was what they saw as an inversion of this rule, where Prospero had imposed his own, alien language as the language of power. There was no sense in which they felt that English *per se* was superior. Further evidence that they saw language as more than a means of communication, as saturated with issues of cultural power, can be found in Sunil's comment: '*Caliban, yeah, he's got his own religion and he should speak his own language if he wants.*' Here he relates language intimately to religion as twin sites of identity. In two separate studies (1993: 29–31 and 2000: 221),[14] Nesbitt found that the terms 'language' and 'religion' could almost be used synonomously among Hindu and Sikh children. When pressed, the children in Interview 1 saw evidence of religion chiefly in Caliban's food – the fishbones, crust of bread and bottle of wine in his cave (5:2c) and cited the Hindu abstinence from beef as the comparative example from which they drew the analogy.[15] This sensitivity was all the more interesting to me as these were unintentional signifiers of religion on my part. Sunil identified a further problem for Caliban, if these scraps were being fed to him by Prospero. '*And Caliban, yeah, whenever he has to eat, yeah, if there's something like he's not allowed to eat in his religion, yeah, he might just have to eat it because Prospero doesn't know what he eats, he just, like, he doesn't learn from him.*' Implicit here is a belief that Prospero, despite his position of dominance, ought consciously to learn the cultural traditions of Caliban and respect them.

Perhaps the most interesting responses to Caliban came when considering his attack on Miranda. In the play it is evidently an attempted rape. In our drama, as in the play, it was referred to, not enacted, and described as a sequence of three actions: Caliban attempting to kiss Miranda; Miranda slapping Caliban; Caliban punching Miranda. The whole class – boys as well as girls – appeared to be clear that Caliban was in the wrong here (5:4e) but the children interviewed had different points to make. Nasreen, despite the pity she had expressed earlier for Caliban, spoke particularly harshly about him here.

> **Miranda is right. Caliban is her father's slave and she shouldn't believe Caliban because he lives in an old tatty cave so good that she slapped him so he can never do anything to her.**

Of course, Nasreen could here be simply identifying with the disgust voiced by Miranda (5:2c). However, her own, animated virulence could be influenced by a perception of Caliban as being of lower caste. Nesbitt's study (1997)[16] of young

British Punjabis' and Gujaratis' perceptions of caste was carried out in the Hindu and Sikh communities of Nottingham and Coventry between 1979 and 1995. She discovered that caste persisted in being seen as relevant particularly in the matter of marriage within the Punjabi community. Shaw, too, found in her study that the boundaries of caste or *biradari* were significant considerations among Pakistani Muslim communities in the case of marriage (2000: 125–34). If my interpretation is correct, then a cultural tradition could be reinforcing Nasreen's gendered feelings of personal disgust and thus deepening her empathy for Miranda.

Paramjeet and Sunil, although not condoning Caliban's actions, did see the incident as possibly stemming from a misunderstanding.

> P: Caliban didn't know what's right or wrong cos he was on his planet. He'd never been to earth. He didn't know what people on earth do. It was a big mistake.
>
> S: Caliban, yeah, in his language, he might have understood that if you kiss someone, yeah, you're welcoming them. He might have thought that.[17]
>
> P: But Miranda didn't know he was going to kiss her. Any girl wouldn't like it if you just kissed her. Because it's two people from two different planets and they don't know each other's rules. You have to know each other's rules.

These comments articulate a strong sensitivity to issues of cultural negotiation. The boys see the source of Caliban's trouble in a mutual lack of multiple cultural competence between himself and Miranda, an awareness, I am tempted to think, enhanced by their own demonstrable possession of it.

The children's responses to magic

Magic and technology fused in our drama, as they do in the genre of science fiction. Prospero's staff was able to freeze anyone it was pointed at and, in the unrevised version of the drama, as Prospero, I handled the planet's rocks with ritualistic reverence, encouraging the children to sense their magical vibrations when selecting a particular rock whose power would repair their work stations (5:5g). The children were more than willing to join in this game of magic and, indeed, were able to use it effectively as a source of dramatic tension. Paramjeet, in particular, found in the link between magic and power his key avenue of engagement in the unfolding drama. He needed no prompting to understand the meaning behind Antonio's recorded message (5:2d) *'When Antonio made his call, it must have been Prospero using his magic powers and he just froze Antonio there.'* While hot-seating (5:3b) he cheekily asked Caliban if he might learn his language so that he could take power over the planet himself; and in (5:4b) he again expressed his desire to overthrow Prospero through a plan to freeze him with his own staff. This engagement was both reflective of and channelled by the particular job he had chosen to apply for – a ship's scientist, with a specified interest in space rocks. At the time of the crash he had, in fact, been experimenting and wrote in his report (5:1g) *'The rocks scattered and a few broke it had just ruined my experiment. I will have to search for more rocks.'*

Paramjeet, like many children of his age, is an avid reader of *Harry Potter* and owns the DVDs of the two recent *Lord of the Rings* films. These may well have helped him engage with the magical elements but there were many other possible avenues of access for the children in this class. When I asked in Interview 2 about stories they had been read when young, some children readily recalled the traditional, western stories of enchantment, fairy tales and the like, but there was also a rich vein of Punjabi stories, from the Muslim tradition, in particular. They shared with me tales of jinns, supernatural creatures of evil who hid in trees at sunset, rode black horses at night, and evidently provided them with a delicious thrill of terror. One girl told me of a 'marble' she had seen on a visit to Pakistan.

> *If you crack it the jinn gets out. It's from a necklace and inside there's a hole, you see something black there. Someone picks it up and breaks it and it comes out and its green.*

This girl for one did not need the help of *Harry Potter* to access the magical elements of our drama, where supernatural power, too, existed in rocks, in the very fabric of the land, as it does on Shakespeare's enchanted island.

Conclusion

Throughout this evaluation, I have been conscious of the danger of imposing an exotic reading of 'otherness' on these children. So let me reiterate that what I have offered is no more than a speculative analysis as to how their understanding of the drama *might* have been framed by the Asian and religious strands of their identities. If, as Nesbitt states, we should understand identity as 'constituted of interpretive narratives, ongoing and shifting, arising from successive encounters' (1998: 196), then metaphors of flux rather than stability are needed to help us appreciate how identity influences action. Nesbitt reminds us that our narratives of identity not only differentiate us from others but also differ at various points in our lives. She draws upon Paul Ricoeur in stating that 'identity is not in opposition to either diversity or plurality . . . personal identity is a history – or story – and, as such, it is an interpretation' (ibid: 191). Here the concept of 'multiple cultural competence' and the aims and strategies of drama education can be seen as comfortable partners. As Carasso (1996)[18] has argued, in drama, at any one time, there are multiple ways in which identity is being played with. If we return to Nasreen in (5:5b), she, Nasreen, was playing Prospero; a female, she was playing a male; a daughter, she was playing a father; a child, she was playing an adult. For this short period of time she was dialoguing with a teacher who was playing her daughter; an adult who was playing an adolescent; an authority figure who was playing her ward. At a deeper, cultural level, she, a British-born South Asian Muslim, was playing a white European Christian opposite a white European Christian. Within such play, multiple cultural competence can not only be articulated but also tried out and developed. The ambivalence and fluidity of Shakespeare's dilemmas can be seen to parallel the cultural complexity through which these children negotiate their lives. As such his stories and his words can be seen as fertile ground for such articulation and development.

Notes

1 Primary National Strategy, *Speaking, Listening, Learning*, DfES reference 0625/6/7–2003 G, 2003.

2 QCA, *Teaching Speaking and Listening at Key Stages 1 and 2*, 1999.

3 Arts Council of England, *Drama in Schools* (second edition), 2003.

4 *Drama and Diversity: A Pluralistic Perspective for Educational Drama*, Portsmouth, NH, Heinemann, 2000. See chapter 4.

5 See www.ofsted.gov.uk/publications

6 Pat's understanding of boys' and girls' play is supported by research. See Carol Gilligan, *In a Different Voice*, Cambridge, MA, Harvard University Press, 1982.

7 E. Nesbitt, 'British, Asian and Hindu: Identity, Self-Narration and the Ethnographic Interview', *Journal of Beliefs and Values*, vol. 19, no. 2, 1998.

8 A. Shaw, *Kinship and Continuity: Pakistani Families in Britain*, Amsterdam, Harwood Academic Publishers, 2000, p. 188.

9 G. Singh, *Immortal Lovers: Tender Tales of Great Love*, New Delhi, Sterling Paperbacks, 1973.

10 Shaw (2000: 139) presents the findings of her survey of the marriage patterns of 70 young Pakistani muslims in Oxford between 1985 and 2000. 53 (or 76%) were married to relatives.

11 Information provided in conversation with Eleanor Nesbitt.

12 This is his own spelling of the Punjabi, meaning 'No, *you* carry them!'

13 Information provided in conversation with Eleanor Nesbitt.

14 R. Jackson and E. Nesbitt, *Hindu Children in Britain*, Stoke on Trent, Trentham Books, 1993; E. Nesbitt, *Religious Lives of Sikh Children: A Coventry Based Study*, Leeds, University of Leeds, 2000.

15 Cf. E. Nesbitt, '"Being Religious Shows in Your Food": Young British Hindus and Vegetarianism', in T.S. Rukmani (ed.), *Hindu Diaspora: Global Perspectives*, Montreal, Concordia University, 1999. The quote in the title of this article is taken from a young Gujarati.

16 E. Nesbitt, '"We Are All Equal": Young British Punjabis' and Gujuratis' Perceptions of Caste', in T.S. Rukmani (ed.), *Hindu Diaspora: Global Perspectives*, Montreal, Concordia University, 1999.

17 Note once again Sunil's conflation of language with another aspect of cultural identity, this time social custom.

18 J.-C. Carasso, 'Identity and Dialogue', in *Drama, Culture and Empowerment: The IDEA Dialogues*, Brisbane, IDEA Publications, 1996.

Drama conventions and games used in this book

Acting out   This is when children improvise around a situation, often in small groups. The intention is not necessarily for them to show their work at the end. If you do want this to be a prelude to some small performance, then see the section on **performance** below.

Collective role   The role of a character is played by more than one child simultaneously. Each child might express a different aspect of the character's personality.

Dramatic play   Children play quite freely while remaining in role throughout. Often the groups can be quite fluid here, especially when the class as a whole are involved in the activity.

Forum theatre   Individual members of the class are chosen to enact a particular scene. The rest of the class observe but both actors and observers can stop the action at any point to ask for or give guidance as to how the scene might be developed.

Hot-seating   Someone (either teacher or child) assumes a role and is questioned by the rest of the group. The role may be signalled by sitting in a particular seat (the 'hot seat') or perhaps by wearing an item of costume or holding a particular artefact.

Line of allegiance   At some point in a drama the teacher asks children to form a line according to their opinion or feelings about a particular character or event. 'If you feel a lot of sympathy for X at this point, stand at this side of the room; if you feel no sympathy at all, stand at the opposite side. If your feelings are not that extreme, place yourself in between at an appropriate place in the line.'

Meeting in role   The whole class is in role as a group that needs to meet to hear news, report on progress or make decisions. The teacher may or may not be in role with the class depending on whether she needs to influence the direction the meeting takes.

Mime   This can range from simple, improvised movement to more carefully crafted uses of movement and gesture. It may be accompanied and supported by teacher narration.

Narration   The teacher may use narration to introduce, link or conclude action. It might be used to slow and intensify action; it may mark the passage of time; or it may introduce the next stage of a drama.

Performance   There will be times in drama lessons when you judge it desirable for children to work in groups and craft their ideas into a **short play**. With primary aged children, this is best kept very short and they will benefit from very clear structures and points of focus. It is often a good idea for groups to perform in sequence with no talking or moving other than from the performers themselves until all groups have finished. This introduction of performance discipline helps children respect their own and one another's work.

Sculpt/model   A child volunteers to be the clay while another child sculpts or models the clay into their idea of how a particular character might appear at a certain moment in the drama. It is often a good idea to encourage a number of different interpretations.

Shadow role   Here the teacher's role is one where she speaks from within the drama in a purely enabling way. She is in the background, an enabler, someone able to ask questions and guide children towards areas of decision but her role is never the subject of any dramatic focus itself.

Sound collage   Sounds are made, often by the whole class using voice, body and/or instruments, either to accompany actions or to create atmosphere.

Still image/tableau   Groups work to create an image of a moment in time using their own bodies. Often it will represent people 'frozen' in the middle of some action but it may represent a more abstract idea.

Storytelling   Exactly what it says! You can use your storytelling skills to interest children in stories that you want them to work on and you can also use them to move the plot along at points within a drama, perhaps in role.

Teacher in role   The teacher takes a full part in the drama, often using her role to manage the drama from within the action. Teacher roles can have a variety of statuses, offering different power relationships within the group. A simple item of costume or a prop can help children understand when you are in or out of role.

GAMES

'Huggy'   Children move through space. When the teacher calls 'Huggy Three' they must all get into threes and form a group hug. At 'Huggy Five' they get into fives, etc. This is a good game to help get children into mixed groups that are not specifically friendship-based.

'Keeper of the Keys'   The children sit in a circle and a volunteer sits blindfolded on a chair in the centre with a rolled up piece of sugar paper in their hand. A large key or other object (such as a book of spells) is placed under the chair. A child in the circle volunteers to attempt to retrieve the object. If the keeper in the centre manages to hit the child with the paper, they must return to the circle and another child can have a try. Silence provides the tension for this very popular game.

'**The Wizard and the Maze**'   The class is organized into three or four neat lines, with children at arm's length from one another. These lines form the walls of the maze and are able to change from being organized lengthways to breadthways, simply by each child moving their right arm from touching the shoulder of the child next to them to the shoulder of the child in front. The pursuer and the pursued are placed at a suitable distance within the maze at the start of the game. Neither is allowed to run through the wall at any time. When the pursuer appears to be getting close to the pursued, the teacher can call 'Change!' at which point the walls change formation, as described above.

'**Through the Magic Forest**'   Half the class are the trees of the forest, half the class are attempting to travel through it without being touched by the trees. The trees are rooted to the ground but their branches (i.e. the children's arms) can move and they try to touch as many of those travelling through the forest as they can.

Establishing a drama contract

A drama contract need not be written down. It is more a case of children under-standing what different things are expected of them when they work in drama as opposed to, say, a literacy or numeracy lesson. The following principles may help you.

- Introduce the idea of pretending with the children and establish that we all know how to pretend. A game such as throwing and catching an imaginary ball around a circle can help with this.

- Discuss with children how we can be someone else and somewhere else when we pretend. Establish with them that, when they pretend, you will, too. If you are going to use some props or costume, show them in advance and get the children to think who you might be without giving too much away.

- Establish clear procedures so that children understand when you and they are in and out of role. The 'Magic Chair' can be very helpful here. Tell children that whatever they are doing, if you sit on that chair they are to come and sit quietly in front of you. This is a particularly effective strategy as it has a game-like quality to it and children enjoy waiting to see who will be the last to notice.

- Be very clear about space. If you are working in a large hall, you may wish to limit the space children are to work in. If you are working in a classroom, you may wish to have children walk through the space and see how there is enough of it for all of them if they share it carefully.

- Ensure that children understand some rules of group work. Make sure they understand that they will sometimes be able to choose their own groups; that sometimes you will choose them; that sometimes they will work in mixed groups and sometimes in single sex groups. When they are in groups, give children a clearly defined space to work in. The challenge here is for them not to be distracted by what children in other groups are doing.

Note: It is generally better to present these as challenges rather than rules: 'Let's see if we can do this . . .' rather than 'You have to do this . . .' In this way, when children have performed well in any of these areas, you can praise them at the end of the lesson.

Children with individual needs may well need additional help or guidance. Autistic children, for example, will need you to explain to them individually and in advance the kind of activities that are going to happen, in particular when you will be working within the fiction.

Index

Printed in the United Kir
by Lightning Source UK
133649UK00006B/13-2